CRACKING THE CODE

BEHIND ENEMY LINES

E. G. WHITE

CRACKING
THE CODE
BEHIND ENEMY LINES

E. G. WHITE

Remnant
Publications

Coldwater MI 49036
www.remnantpublications.com

Copyright © 2008
All Rights Reserved
Printed in the USA

Published by
Remnant Publications
649 East Chicago Road
Coldwater MI 49036
517-279-1304
www.remnantpublications.com

This book is a portion of a work originally published
under the title, *The Great Controversy.*

All Bible Scripture is taken from the King James Version, Revised Version,
or American Revised Version.

Cover design by David Berthiaume
Text design by Greg Solie • AltamontGraphics.com

ISBN 978-1-933291-40-6

Contents

One

—The Origin of Evil—

To many minds the origin of sin and the reason for its existence are a source of great perplexity. They see the work of evil, with its terrible results of woe and desolation, and they question how all this can exist under the sovereignty of One who is infinite in wisdom, in power, and in love. Here is a mystery of which they find no explanation. And in their uncertainty and doubt they are blinded to truths plainly revealed in God's word and essential to salvation. There are those who, in their inquiries concerning the existence of sin, endeavor to search into that which God has never revealed; hence they find no solution of their difficulties; and such as are actuated by a disposition to doubt and cavil seize upon this as an excuse for rejecting the words of Holy Writ. Others, however, fail of a satisfactory understanding of the great problem of evil, from the fact that tradition and misinterpretation have obscured the teaching of the Bible concerning the character of God, the nature of His government, and the principles of His dealing with sin.

It is impossible to explain the origin of sin so as to give a reason for its existence. Yet enough may be understood concerning both the origin and the final disposition of sin to make fully manifest the justice and benevolence of God in all His dealings with evil. Nothing is more plainly taught in Scripture than that God was in no wise responsible for the entrance of sin; that there was no arbitrary withdrawal of divine grace, no deficiency in the divine government, that gave occasion for the uprising of rebellion. Sin is an intruder, for whose presence no reason can be given. It is mysterious, unaccountable; to excuse it is to defend it. Could excuse for it be found, or cause be shown for its existence, it would cease to be sin. Our only definition of sin is that given in the word of God; it is "the transgression of the law;" it is the outworking of a principle at war with the great law of love which is the foundation of the divine government.

Before the entrance of evil there was peace and joy throughout the universe. All was in perfect harmony with the Creator's will. Love for God was supreme, love for one another impartial. Christ the Word, the Only Begotten of God, was one with the eternal Father,—one in nature, in character, and in purpose,—the only being in all the universe that could enter into all the counsels and purposes of God. By Christ the Father wrought in the creation of all heavenly beings. "By Him were all things created, that are in heaven, ... whether they be thrones, or dominions, or principalities, or powers" (Colossians 1:16); and to Christ, equally with the Father, all heaven gave allegiance.

The law of love being the foundation of the government of God, the happiness of all created beings depended upon their perfect accord with its great principles of righteousness. God desires from all His creatures the service of love—homage that springs from an intelligent appreciation of His character. He takes no pleasure in a forced allegiance, and to all He grants freedom of will, that they may render Him voluntary service.

But there was one that chose to pervert this freedom. Sin originated with him who, next to Christ, had been most honored of God and who stood highest in power and glory among the inhabitants of heaven. Before his fall, Lucifer was first of the covering cherubs, holy and undefiled. "Thus saith the Lord God; Thou sealest up the sum, full of wisdom, and perfect in beauty. Thou hast been in Eden the garden of God; every precious stone was thy covering. ...Thou art the anointed cherub that covereth; and I have set thee so: thou wast upon the holy mountain of God; thou hast walked up and down in the midst of the stones of fire. Thou wast perfect in thy ways from the day that thou wast created, till iniquity was found in thee." Ezekiel 28:12-15.

Lucifer might have remained in favor with God, beloved and honored by all the angelic host, exercising his noble powers to bless others and to glorify his Maker. But, says the prophet, "Thine heart was lifted up because of thy beauty, thou hast corrupted thy wisdom by reason of thy brightness." Verse 17. Little by little, Lucifer came to indulge a desire for self-exaltation. "Thou hast set thine heart as the heart of God." "Thou hast said, ... I will exalt my throne above the stars of God: I will sit also upon the mount of the congregation. ... I will ascend above the heights of the clouds; I will be like the Most High." Verse 6; Isaiah 14:13, 14. Instead of seeking to make God supreme in the affections and allegiance of His creatures, it was Lucifer's endeavor to win their service and homage to himself. And coveting the honor which the infinite Father had bestowed upon His Son, this prince of angels aspired to power which it was the prerogative of Christ alone to wield.

All heaven had rejoiced to reflect the Creator's glory and to show forth His praise. And while God was thus honored, all had been peace and gladness. But a note of discord now marred the celestial harmonies. The service and exaltation of self, contrary to the Creator's plan, awakened forebodings of evil in minds to whom God's glory was supreme. The heavenly councils pleaded with Lucifer. The Son of God presented before him the greatness, the goodness, and the justice of the Creator, and the sacred, unchanging nature of His law. God Himself had established the order of heaven; and in departing from it, Lucifer would dishonor his Maker, and bring ruin upon himself. But the warning, given in infinite love and mercy, only aroused a spirit of resistance. Lucifer allowed jealousy of Christ to prevail, and he became the more determined.

Pride in his own glory nourished the desire for supremacy. The high honors conferred upon Lucifer were not appreciated as the gift of God and called forth no gratitude to the Creator. He gloried in his brightness and exaltation, and aspired to be equal with God. He was beloved and reverenced by the heavenly host. Angels delighted to execute his commands, and he was clothed with wisdom and glory above them all. Yet the Son of God was the acknowledged Sovereign of heaven, one in power and authority with the Father. In all the councils of God, Christ was a participant, while Lucifer was not permitted thus to enter into the divine purposes. "Why," questioned this mighty angel, "should Christ have the supremacy? Why is He thus honored above Lucifer?"

Leaving his place in the immediate presence of God, Lucifer went forth to diffuse the spirit of discontent among the angels. Working with mysterious secrecy, and for a time concealing his real purpose under an appearance of reverence for God, he endeavored to excite dissatisfaction concerning the laws that governed heavenly beings, intimating that they imposed an unnecessary restraint. Since their natures were holy, he urged that the angels should obey the dictates of their own will. He sought to create sympathy for himself by representing that

God had dealt unjustly with him in bestowing supreme honor upon Christ. He claimed that in aspiring to greater power and honor he was not aiming at self-exaltation, but was seeking to secure liberty for all the inhabitants of heaven, that by this means they might attain to a higher state of existence.

God in His great mercy bore long with Lucifer. He was not immediately degraded from his exalted station when he first indulged the spirit of discontent, nor even when he began to present his false claims before the loyal angels. Long was he retained in heaven. Again and again he was offered pardon on condition of repentance and submission. Such efforts as only infinite love and wisdom could devise were made to convince him of his error. The spirit of discontent had never before been known in heaven. Lucifer himself did not at first see whither he was drifting; he did not understand the real nature of his feelings. But as his dissatisfaction was proved to be without cause, Lucifer was convinced that he was in the wrong, that the divine claims were just, and that he ought to acknowledge them as such before all heaven. Had he done this, he might have saved himself and many angels. He had not at this time fully cast off his allegiance to God. Though he had forsaken his position as covering cherub, yet if he had been willing to return to God, acknowledging the Creator's wisdom, and satisfied to fill the place appointed him in God's great plan, he would have been reinstated in his office. But pride forbade him to submit. He persistently defended his own course, maintained that he had no need of repentance, and fully committed himself, in the great controversy, against his Maker.

All the powers of his master mind were now bent to the work of deception, to secure the sympathy of the angels that had been under his command. Even the fact that Christ had warned and counseled him was perverted to serve his traitorous designs. To those whose loving trust bound them most closely to him, Satan had represented that he was wrongly judged, that his position was not respected, and that his liberty was to be abridged. From misrepresentation of the words of Christ he passed to prevarication and direct falsehood, accusing the Son of God of a design to humiliate him before the inhabitants of heaven. He sought also to make a false issue between himself and the loyal angels. All whom he could not subvert and bring fully to his side he accused of indifference to the interests of heavenly beings. The very work which he himself was doing he charged upon those who remained true to God. And to sustain his charge of God's injustice toward him, he resorted to misrepresentation of the words and acts of the Creator. It was his policy to perplex the angels with subtle arguments concerning the purposes of God. Everything that was simple he shrouded in mystery, and by artful perversion cast doubt upon the plainest statements of Jehovah. His high position, in such close connection with the divine administration, gave greater force to his representations, and many were induced to unite with him in rebellion against Heaven's authority.

God in His wisdom permitted Satan to carry forward his work, until the spirit of disaffection ripened into active revolt. It was necessary for his plans to be fully developed, that their true nature and tendency might be seen by all. Lucifer, as the anointed cherub, had been highly exalted; he was greatly loved by the heavenly beings, and his influence over them was strong. God's government included not only the inhabitants of heaven, but of all the worlds that He had created; and Satan thought that if he could carry the angels of heaven with him in rebellion, he could carry also the other worlds. He had artfully presented his side of the question, employing sophistry and fraud to secure his objects. His power to deceive was very great, and by disguising himself in a cloak of falsehood he had gained an advantage. Even the loyal angels could not fully discern his character or see to what his work was leading.

Satan had been so highly honored, and all his acts were so clothed with mystery, that it was difficult to disclose to the angels the true nature of his work. Until fully developed, sin would not appear the evil thing it was. Heretofore it had had no place in the universe of God, and holy beings had no conception of its nature and malignity. They could not discern the terrible consequences that would result from setting aside the divine law. Satan had, at first, concealed his work under a specious profession of loyalty to God. He claimed to be seeking to promote the honor of God, the stability of His government, and the good of all the inhabitants of heaven. While instilling discontent into the minds of the angels under him, he had artfully made it appear that he was seeking to remove dissatisfaction. When he urged that changes be made in the order and laws of God's government, it was under the pretense that these were necessary in order to preserve harmony in heaven.

In His dealing with sin, God could employ only righteousness and truth. Satan could use what God could not—flattery and deceit. He had sought to falsify the word of God and had misrepresented His plan of government before the angels, claiming that God was not just in laying laws and rules upon the inhabitants of heaven; that in requiring submission and obedience from His creatures, He was seeking merely the exaltation of Himself. Therefore it must be demonstrated before the inhabitants of heaven, as well as of all the worlds, that God's government was just, His law perfect. Satan had made it appear that he himself was seeking to promote the good of the universe. The true character of the usurper, and his real object, must be understood by all. He must have time to manifest himself by his wicked works.

The discord which his own course had caused in heaven, Satan charged upon the law and government of God. All evil he declared to be the result of the divine administration. He claimed that it was his own object to improve upon the statutes of Jehovah. Therefore it was necessary that he should demonstrate the nature of his claims, and show the working out of his proposed changes in the divine law. His own work must condemn him. Satan had claimed from the first that he was not in rebellion. The whole universe must see the deceiver unmasked.

Even when it was decided that he could no longer remain in heaven, Infinite Wisdom did not destroy Satan. Since the service of love can alone be acceptable to God, the allegiance of His creatures must rest upon a conviction of His justice and benevolence. The inhabitants of heaven and of other worlds, being unprepared to comprehend the nature or consequences of sin, could not then have seen the justice and mercy of God in the destruction of Satan. Had he been immediately blotted from existence, they would have served God from fear rather than from love. The influence of the deceiver would not have been fully destroyed, nor would the spirit of rebellion have been utterly eradicated. Evil must be permitted to come to maturity. For the good of the entire universe through ceaseless ages Satan must more fully develop his principles, that his charges against the divine government might be seen in their true light by all created beings, that the justice and mercy of God and the immutability of His law might forever be placed beyond all question.

Satan's rebellion was to be a lesson to the universe through all coming ages, a perpetual testimony to the nature and terrible results of sin. The working out of Satan's rule, its effects upon both men and angels, would show what must be the fruit of setting aside the divine authority.

It would testify that with the existence of God's government and His law is bound up the well-being of all the creatures He has made. Thus the history of this terrible experiment of rebellion was to be a perpetual safeguard to all holy intelligences, to prevent them from being deceived as to the nature of transgression, to save them from committing sin and suffering its punishments.

To the very close of the controversy in heaven the great usurper continued to justify himself. When it was announced that with all his sympathizers he must be expelled from the abodes of bliss, then the rebel leader boldly avowed his contempt for the Creator's law. He reiterated his claim that angels needed no control, but should be left to follow their own will, which would ever guide them right. He denounced the divine statutes as a restriction of their liberty and declared that it was his purpose to secure the abolition of law; that, freed from this restraint, the hosts of heaven might enter upon a more exalted, more glorious state of existence.

With one accord, Satan and his host threw the blame of their rebellion wholly upon Christ, declaring that if they had not been re-proved, they would never have rebelled. Thus stubborn and defiant in their disloyalty, seeking vainly to overthrow the government of God, yet blasphemously claiming to be themselves the innocent victims of oppressive power, the archrebel and all his sympathizers were at last banished from heaven.

The same spirit that prompted rebellion in heaven still inspires re-bellion on earth. Satan has continued with men the same policy which he pursued with the angels. His spirit now reigns in the children of disobedience. Like him they seek to break down the restraints of the law of God and promise men liberty through transgression of its precepts. Reproof of sin still arouses the spirit of hatred and resistance. When God's messages of warning are brought home to the conscience, Satan leads men to justify themselves and to seek the sympathy of others in their course of sin. Instead of correcting their errors, they excite indigna-tion against the reprover, as if he were the sole cause of difficulty. From the days of righteous Abel to our own time such is the spirit which has been displayed toward those who dare to condemn sin.

By the same misrepresentation of the character of God as he had practiced in heaven, causing Him to be regarded as severe and tyran-nical, Satan induced man to sin. And having succeeded thus far, he declared that God's unjust restrictions had led to man's fall, as they had led to his own rebellion.

But the Eternal One Himself proclaims His character: "The Lord God, merciful and gracious, long-suffering, and abundant in goodness and truth, keeping mercy for thousands, forgiving iniquity and transgression and sin, and that will by no means clear the guilty." Exodus 34:6, 7.

In the banishment of Satan from heaven, God declared His justice and maintained the honor of His throne. But when man had sinned through yielding to the deceptions of this apostate spirit, God gave an evidence of His love by yielding up His only-begotten Son to die for the fallen race. In the atonement the character of God is revealed. The mighty argument of the cross demonstrates to the whole universe that the course of sin which Lucifer had chosen was in no wise chargeable upon the government of God.

In the contest between Christ and Satan, during the Saviour's earthly ministry, the character of the great deceiver was unmasked. Nothing could so effectually have uprooted Satan from the affections of the heavenly angels and the whole loyal universe as did his cruel warfare upon the world's Redeemer. The daring blasphemy of his demand that Christ should pay him homage, his presumptuous boldness in bearing Him to the mountain summit and the pinnacle of the temple, the malicious intent betrayed in urging Him to cast Himself down from the dizzy height, the unsleeping malice that hunted Him from place to place, inspiring the hearts of priests and people to reject His love, and at the last to cry, "Crucify Him! crucify Him!—all this excited the amazement and indignation of the universe.

It was Satan that prompted the world's rejection of Christ. The prince of evil exerted all his power and cunning to destroy Jesus; for he saw that the Saviour's mercy and love, His compassion and pitying tenderness, were representing to the world the character of God. Satan contested every claim put forth by the Son of God and employed men as his agents to fill the Saviour's life with suffering and sorrow. The sophistry and falsehood by which he had sought to hinder the work of Jesus, the hatred manifested through the children of disobedience, his cruel accusations against Him whose life was one of unexampled goodness, all sprang from deep-seated revenge. The pent-up fires of envy and malice, hatred and revenge, burst forth on Calvary against the Son of God, while all heaven gazed upon the scene in silent horror.

When the great sacrifice had been consummated, Christ ascended on high, refusing the adoration of angels until He had presented the request: "I will that they also, whom Thou hast given Me, be with Me where I am." John 17:24. Then with inexpressible love and power came forth the answer from the Father's throne: "Let all the angels of God worship Him." Hebrews 1:6. Not a stain rested upon Jesus. His humiliation ended, His sacrifice completed, there was given unto Him a name that is above every name.

Now the guilt of Satan stood forth without excuse. He had revealed his true character as a liar and a murderer. It was seen that the very same spirit with which he ruled the children of men, who were under his power, he would have manifested had he been permitted to control the inhabitants of heaven. He had claimed that the transgression of God's law would bring liberty and exaltation; but it was seen to result in bondage and degradation.

Satan's lying charges against the divine character and government appeared in their true light. He had accused God of seeking merely the exaltation of Himself in requiring submission and obedience from His creatures, and had declared that, while the Creator exacted self-denial from all others, He Himself practiced no self-denial and made no sacrifice. Now it was seen that for the salvation of a fallen and sinful race, the Ruler of the universe had made the greatest sacrifice which love could make; for "God was in Christ, reconciling the world unto Himself." 2 Corinthians 5:19. It was seen, also, that while Lucifer had opened the door for the entrance of sin by his desire for honor and supremacy, Christ had, in order to destroy sin, humbled Himself and become obedient unto death.

God had manifested His abhorrence of the principles of rebellion. All heaven saw His justice revealed, both in the condemnation of Satan and in the redemption of man. Lucifer had declared that if the law of God was changeless, and its penalty could not be remitted, every transgressor must be forever debarred from the Creator's favor. He had claimed that the sinful race were placed beyond redemption and were therefore his rightful prey. But the death of Christ was an argument in man's behalf that could not be overthrown. The penalty of the law fell upon Him who was equal with God, and man was free to accept the righteousness of Christ and by a life of penitence and humiliation to triumph, as the Son of God had triumphed, over the power of Satan. Thus God is just and yet the justifier of all who believe in Jesus.

But it was not merely to accomplish the redemption of man that Christ came to the earth to suffer and to die. He came to "magnify the law" and to "make it honorable." Not alone that the inhabitants of this world might regard the law as it should be regarded; but it was to demonstrate to all the worlds of the universe that God's law is unchangeable. Could its claims have been set aside, then the Son of God need not have yielded up His life to atone for its transgression. The death of Christ proves it immutable. And the sacrifice to which infinite love impelled the Father and the Son, that sinners might be redeemed, demonstrates to all the universe—what nothing less than this plan of atonement could have sufficed to do—that justice and mercy are the foundation of the law and government of God.

In the final execution of the judgment it will be seen that no cause for sin exists. When the Judge of all the earth shall demand of Satan, "Why hast thou rebelled against Me, and robbed Me of the subjects of My kingdom?" the originator of evil can render no excuse. Every mouth will be stopped, and all the hosts of rebellion will be speechless.

The cross of Calvary, while it declares the law immutable, proclaims to the universe that the wages of sin is death. In the Saviour's expiring cry, "It is finished," the death knell of Satan was rung. The great controversy which had been so long in progress was then decided, and the final eradication of evil was made certain. The Son of God passed through the portals of the tomb, that "through death He might destroy him that had the power of death, that is, the devil." Hebrews 2:14. Lucifer's desire for self-exaltation had led him to say: "I will exalt my throne above the stars of God: ... I will be like the Most High." God declares: "I will bring thee to ashes upon the earth, ... and never shalt thou be any more." Isaiah 14:13, 14; Ezekiel 28:18, 19. When "the day cometh, that shall burn as an oven;. ... all the proud, yea, and all that do wickedly, shall be stubble: and the day that cometh shall burn them up, saith the Lord of hosts, that it shall leave them neither root nor branch." Malachi 4:1.

The whole universe will have become witnesses to the nature and results of sin. And its utter extermination, which in the beginning would have brought fear to angels and dishonor to God, will now vindicate His love and establish His honor before the universe of beings who delight to do His will, and in whose heart is His law. Never will evil again be manifest. Says the word of God: "Affliction shall not rise up the second time." Nahum 1:9. The law of God, which Satan has reproached as the yoke of bondage, will be honored as the law of liberty. A tested and proved creation will never again be turned from allegiance to Him whose character has been fully manifested before them as fathomless love and infinite wisdom.

Two

—Enmity Between Man and Satan—

"I will put enmity between thee and the woman, and between thy seed and her seed; it shall bruise thy head, and thou shalt bruise his heel." Genesis 3:15. The divine sentence pronounced against Satan after the fall of man was also a prophecy, embracing all the ages to the close of time and foreshadowing the great conflict to engage all the races of men who should live upon the earth.

God declares: "I will put enmity." This enmity is not naturally entertained. When man transgressed the divine law, his nature became evil, and he was in harmony, and not at variance, with Satan. There exists naturally no enmity between sinful man and the originator of sin. Both became evil through apostasy. The apostate is never at rest, except as he obtains sympathy and support by inducing others to follow his example. For this reason fallen angels and wicked men unite in desperate companionship. Had not God specially interposed, Satan and man would have entered into an alliance against Heaven; and instead of cherishing enmity against Satan, the whole human family would have been united in opposition to God.

Satan tempted man to sin, as he had caused angels to rebel, that he might thus secure co-operation in his warfare against Heaven. There was no dissension between himself and the fallen angels as regards their hatred of Christ; while on all other points there was discord, they were firmly united in opposing the authority of the Ruler of the universe. But when Satan heard the declaration that enmity should exist between himself and the woman, and between his seed and her seed, he knew that his efforts to deprave human nature would be interrupted; that by some means man was to be enabled to resist his power.

Satan's enmity against the human race is kindled because, through Christ, they are the objects of God's love and mercy. He desires to thwart the divine plan for man's redemption, to cast dishonor upon God, by defacing and defiling His handiwork; he would cause grief in heaven and fill the earth with woe and desolation. And he points to all this evil as the result of God's work in creating man.

It is the grace that Christ implants in the soul which creates in man enmity against Satan. Without this converting grace and renewing power, man would continue the captive of Satan, a servant ever ready to do his bidding. But the new principle in the soul creates conflict where hitherto had been peace. The power which Christ imparts enables man to resist the tyrant and usurper. Whoever is seen to abhor sin instead of loving it, whoever resists and conquers those passions that have held sway within, displays the operation of a principle wholly from above.

The antagonism that exists between the spirit of Christ and the spirit of Satan was most strikingly displayed in the world's reception of Jesus. It was not so much because He appeared without worldly wealth, pomp, or grandeur that the Jews were led to reject Him. They saw that He possessed power which would more than compensate for the lack of these outward advantages. But the purity and holiness of Christ called forth against Him the hatred of the ungodly. His life of self-denial and sinless devotion was a perpetual reproof to a proud, sensual people. It was this that evoked enmity against the Son of God. Satan and evil angels joined with evil men. All the energies of apostasy conspired against the Champion of truth.

The same enmity is manifested toward Christ's followers as was manifested toward their Master. Whoever sees the repulsive character of sin, and in strength from above resists temptation, will assuredly arouse the wrath of Satan and his subjects. Hatred of the pure principles of truth, and reproach and persecution of its advocates, will exist as long as sin and sinners remain. The followers of Christ and the servants of Satan cannot harmonize. The offense of the cross has not ceased. "All that will live godly in Christ Jesus shall suffer persecution." 2 Timothy 3:12.

Satan's agents are constantly working under his direction to establish his authority and build up his kingdom in opposition to the government of God. To this end they seek to deceive Christ's followers and allure them from their allegiance. Like their leader, they misconstrue and pervert the Scriptures to accomplish their object. As Satan endeavored to cast reproach upon God, so do his agents seek to malign God's people.

The spirit which put Christ to death moves the wicked to destroy His followers. All this is foreshadowed in that first prophecy: "I will put enmity between thee and the woman, and between thy seed and her seed." And this will continue to the close of time.

Satan summons all his forces and throws his whole power into the combat. Why is it that he meets with no greater resistance? Why are the soldiers of Christ so sleepy and indifferent? Because they have so little real connection with Christ; because they are so destitute of His Spirit. Sin is not to them repulsive and abhorrent, as it was to their Master. They do not meet it, as did Christ, with decisive and determined resistance. They do not realize the exceeding evil and malignity of sin, and they are blinded both to the character and the power of the prince of darkness. There is little enmity against Satan and his works, because there is so great ignorance concerning his power and malice, and the vast extent of his warfare against Christ and His church. Multitudes are deluded here. They do not know that their enemy is a mighty general who controls the minds of evil angels, and that with well-matured plans and skillful movements he is warring against Christ to prevent the salvation of souls. Among professed Christians, and even among ministers of the gospel, there is heard scarcely a reference to Satan, except perhaps an incidental mention in the pulpit. They overlook the evidences of his continual activity and success; they neglect the many warnings of his subtlety; they seem to ignore his very existence.

While men are ignorant of his devices, this vigilant foe is upon their track every moment. He is intruding his presence in every department of the household, in every street of our cities, in the churches, in the national councils, in the courts of justice, perplexing, deceiving, seducing, everywhere ruining the souls and bodies of men, women, and children, breaking up families, sowing hatred, emulation, strife, sedition, murder. And the Christian world seem to regard these things as though God had appointed them and they must exist.

Satan is continually seeking to overcome the people of God by breaking down the barriers which separate them from the world. Ancient Israel were enticed into sin when they ventured into forbidden association with the heathen. In a similar manner are modern Israel led astray. "The god of this world hath blinded the minds of them which believe not, lest the light of the glorious gospel of Christ, who is the image of God, should shine unto them." 2 Corinthians 4:4. All who are not decided followers of Christ are servants of Satan. In the unregenerate heart there is love of sin and a disposition to cherish and excuse it. In the renewed heart there is hatred of sin and determined resistance against it. When Christians choose the society of the ungodly and unbelieving, they expose themselves to temptation. Satan conceals himself from view and stealthily draws his deceptive covering over their eyes. They cannot see that such company is calculated to do them harm; and while all the time assimilating to the world in character, words, and actions, they are becoming more and more blinded.

Conformity to worldly customs converts the church to the world; it never converts the world to Christ. Familiarity with sin will inevitably cause it to appear less repulsive. He who chooses to associate with the servants of Satan will soon cease to fear their master. When in the way of duty we are brought into trial, as was Daniel in the king's court, we may be sure that God will protect us; but if we place ourselves under temptation we shall fall sooner or later.

The tempter often works most successfully through those who are least suspected of being under his control. The possessors of talent and education are admired and honored, as if these qualities could atone for the absence of the fear of God or entitle men to His favor. Talent and culture, considered in themselves, are gifts of God; but when these are made to supply the place of piety, when, instead of bringing the soul nearer to God, they lead away from Him, then they become a curse and a snare. The opinion prevails with many that all which appears like courtesy or refinement must, in some sense, pertain to Christ. Never was there a greater mistake. These qualities should grace the character of every Christian, for they would exert a powerful influence in favor of true religion; but they must be consecrated to God, or they also are a power for evil. Many a man of cultured intellect and pleasant manners, who would not stoop to what is commonly regarded as an immoral act, is but a polished instrument in the hands of Satan. The insidious, deceptive character of his influence and example renders him a more dangerous enemy to the cause of Christ than are those who are ignorant and uncultured.

By earnest prayer and dependence upon God, Solomon obtained the wisdom which excited the wonder and admiration of the world. But when he turned from the Source of his strength, and went forward relying upon himself, he fell a prey to temptation. Then the marvelous powers bestowed on this wisest of kings only rendered him a more effective agent of the adversary of souls.

While Satan is constantly seeking to blind their minds to the fact, let Christians never forget that they "wrestle not against flesh and blood, but against principalities, against powers, against the rulers of the darkness of this world, against wicked spirits in high places." Ephesians 6:12, margin. The inspired warning is sounding down the centuries to our time: "Be sober, be vigilant; because your adversary the devil, as a roaring lion, walketh about, seeking whom he may devour." 1 Peter 5:8. "Put on the whole armor of God, that ye may be able to stand against the wiles of the devil." Ephesians 6:11.

From the days of Adam to our own time, our great enemy has been exercising his power to oppress and destroy. He is now preparing for his last campaign against the church. All who seek to follow Jesus will be brought into conflict with this relentless foe. The more nearly the Christian imitates the divine Pattern, the more surely will he make himself a mark for the attacks of Satan. All who are actively engaged in the cause of God, seeking to unveil the deceptions of the evil one and to present Christ before the people, will be able to join in the testimony of Paul, in which he speaks of serving the Lord with all humility of mind, with many tears and temptations.

Satan assailed Christ with his fiercest and most subtle temptations, but he was repulsed in every conflict. Those battles were fought in our behalf; those victories make it possible for us to conquer. Christ will give strength to all who seek it. No man without his own consent can be overcome by Satan. The tempter has no power to control the will or to force the soul to sin. He may distress, but he cannot contaminate. He can cause agony, but not defilement. The fact that Christ has conquered should inspire His followers with courage to fight manfully the battle against sin and Satan.

Three

—Agency of Evil Spirits—

The connection of the visible with the invisible world, the ministration of angels of God, and the agency of evil spirits, are plainly revealed in the Scriptures, and inseparably interwoven with human history. There is a growing tendency to disbelief in the existence of evil spirits, while the holy angels that "minister for them who shall be heirs of salvation" (Hebrews 1:14) are regarded by many as spirits of the dead. But the Scriptures not only teach the existence of angels, both good and evil, but present unquestionable proof that these are not disembodied spirits of dead men.

Before the creation of man, angels were in existence; for when the foundations of the earth were laid, "the morning stars sang together, and all the sons of God shouted for joy." Job 38:7. After the fall of man, angels were sent to guard the tree of life, and this before a human being had died. Angels are in nature superior to men, for the psalmist says that man was made "a little lower than the angels." Psalm 8:5.

We are informed in Scripture as to the number, and the power and glory, of the heavenly beings, of their connection with the government of God, and also of their relation to the work of redemption. "The Lord hath prepared His throne in the heavens; and His kingdom ruleth over all." And, says the prophet, "I heard the voice of many angels round about the throne." In the presence chamber of the King of kings they wait—"angels, that excel in strength," "ministers of His, that do His pleasure," "hearkening unto the voice of His word." Psalm 103:19-21; Revelation 5:11. Ten thousand times ten thousand and thousands of thousands, were the heavenly messengers beheld by the prophet Daniel. The apostle Paul declared them "an innumerable company." Daniel 7:10; Hebrews 12:22. As God's messengers they go forth, like "the appearance of a flash of lightning," (Ezekiel 1:14), so dazzling their glory, and so swift their flight. The angel that appeared at the Saviour's tomb, his countenance "like lightning, and his raiment white as snow," caused the keepers for fear of him to quake, and they "became as dead men." Matthew 28:3, 4. When Sennacherib, the haughty Assyrian, reproached and blasphemed God, and threatened Israel with destruction, "it came to pass that night, that the angel of the Lord went out, and smote in the camp of the Assyrians an hundred fourscore and five thousand." There were "cut off all the mighty men of valor, and the leaders and captains," from the army of Sennacherib. "So he returned with shame of face to his own land." 2 Kings 19:35; 2 Chronicles 32:21.

Angels are sent on missions of mercy to the children of God. To Abraham, with promises of blessing; to the gates of Sodom, to rescue righteous Lot from its fiery doom; to Elijah, as he was about to perish from weariness and hunger in the desert; to Elisha, with chariots and horses of fire surrounding the little town where he was shut in by his foes; to Daniel, while seeking divine wisdom in the court of a heathen king, or abandoned to become the lions' prey; to Peter, doomed to death in Herod's dungeon; to the prisoners at Philippi; to Paul and his companions in the night of tempest on the sea; to open the mind of Cornelius to receive the gospel; to dispatch Peter with the message of salvation to the Gentile stranger—thus holy angels have, in all ages, ministered to God's people.

A guardian angel is appointed to every follower of Christ. These heavenly watchers shield the righteous from the power of the wicked one. This Satan himself recognized when he said: "Doth Job fear God for nought? Hast not Thou made an hedge about him, and about his house, and about all that he hath on every side?" Job 1:9, 10. The agency by which God protects His people is presented in the words of the psalmist: "The angel of the Lord encampeth round about them that fear Him, and delivereth them." Psalm 34:7. Said the Saviour, speaking of those that believe in Him: "Take heed that ye despise not one of these little ones; for I say unto you, That in heaven their angels do always behold the face of My Father." Matthew 18:10. The angels appointed to minister to the children of God have at all times access to His presence.

Thus God's people, exposed to the deceptive power and unsleeping malice of the prince of darkness, and in conflict with all the forces of evil, are assured of the unceasing guardianship of heavenly angels. Nor is such assurance given without need. If God has granted to His children promise of grace and protection, it is because there are mighty agencies of evil to be met—agencies numerous, determined, and untiring, of whose malignity and power none can safely be ignorant or unheeding.

Evil spirits, in the beginning created sinless, were equal in nature, power, and glory with the holy beings that are now God's messengers. But fallen through sin, they are leagued together for the dishonor of God and the destruction of men. United with Satan in his rebellion, and with him cast out from heaven, they have, through all succeeding ages, co-operated with him in his warfare against the divine authority. We are told in Scripture of their confederacy and government, of their various orders, of their intelligence and subtlety, and of their malicious designs against the peace and happiness of men.

Old Testament history presents occasional mention of their existence and agency; but it was during the time when Christ was upon the earth that evil spirits manifested their power in the most striking manner. Christ had come to enter upon the plan devised for man's redemption, and Satan determined to assert his right to control the world. He had succeeded in establishing idolatry in every part of the earth except the land of Palestine. To the only land that had not fully yielded to the tempter's sway, Christ came to shed upon the people the light of heaven. Here two rival powers claimed supremacy. Jesus was stretching out His arms of love, inviting all who would to find pardon and peace in Him. The hosts of darkness saw that they did not possess unlimited control, and they understood that if Christ's mission should be successful, their rule was soon to end. Satan raged like a chained lion and defiantly exhibited his power over the bodies as well as the souls of men.

The fact that men have been possessed with demons, is clearly stated in the New Testament. The persons thus afflicted were not merely suffering with disease from natural causes. Christ had perfect understanding of that with which He was dealing, and He recognized the direct presence and agency of evil spirits.

A striking example of their number, power, and malignity, and also of the power and mercy of Christ, is given in the Scripture account of the healing of the demoniacs at Gadara. Those wretched maniacs, spurning all restraint, writhing, foaming, raging, were filling the air with their cries, doing violence to themselves, and endangering all who should approach them. Their bleeding and disfigured bodies and distracted minds presented a spectacle well pleasing to the prince of darkness. One of the demons controlling the sufferers declared: "My name is Legion: for we are many." Mark 5:9. In the Roman army a legion consisted of from three to five thousand men. Satan's hosts also are marshaled in companies, and the single company to which these demons belonged numbered no less than a legion.

At the command of Jesus the evil spirits departed from their victims, leaving them calmly sitting at the Saviour's feet, subdued, intelligent, and gentle. But the demons were permitted to sweep a herd of swine into the sea; and to the dwellers of Gadara the loss of these outweighed the blessings which Christ had bestowed, and the divine Healer was entreated to depart. This was the result which Satan designed to secure. By casting the blame of their loss upon Jesus, he aroused the selfish fears of the people and prevented them from listening to His words. Satan is constantly accusing Christians as the cause of loss, misfortune, and suffering, instead of allowing the reproach to fall where it belongs—upon himself and his agents.

But the purposes of Christ were not thwarted. He allowed the evil spirits to destroy the herd of swine as a rebuke to those Jews who were raising these unclean beasts for the sake of gain. Had not Christ restrained the demons, they would have plunged into the sea, not only the swine, but also their keepers and owners. The preservation of both the keepers and the owners was due alone to His power, mercifully exercised for their deliverance. Furthermore, this event was permitted to take place that the disciples might witness the cruel power of Satan upon both man and beast. The Saviour desired His followers to have a knowledge of the foe whom they were to meet, that they might not be deceived and overcome by his devices. It was also His will that the people of that region should behold His power to break the bondage of Satan and release his captives. And though Jesus Himself departed, the men so marvelously delivered, remained to declare the mercy of their Benefactor.

Other instances of a similar nature are recorded in the Scriptures. The daughter of the Syrophoenician woman was grievously vexed with a devil, whom Jesus cast out by His word. Mark 7:26-30. "One possessed with a devil, blind, and dumb" (Matthew 12:22); a youth who had a dumb spirit, that ofttimes "cast him into the fire, and into the waters, to destroy him" (Mark 9:17-27); the maniac who, tormented by "a spirit of an unclean devil" (Luke 4:33-36), disturbed the Sabbath quiet of the synagogue at Capernaum—all were healed by the compassionate Saviour. In nearly every instance, Christ addressed the demon as an intelligent entity, commanding him to come out of his victim and to torment him no more. The worshipers at Capernaum, beholding His mighty power, "were all amazed, and spake among themselves, saying, What a word is this! for with authority and power He commandeth the unclean spirits, and they come out." Luke 4:36.

Those possessed with devils are usually represented as being in a condition of great suffering; yet there were exceptions to this rule. For the sake of obtaining supernatural power, some welcomed the satanic influence. These of course had no conflict with the demons. Of this class were those who possessed the spirit of divination,—Simon Magus, Elymas the sorcerer, and the damsel who followed Paul and Silas at Philippi.

None are in greater danger from the influence of evil spirits than those who, notwithstanding the direct and ample testimony of the Scriptures, deny the existence and agency of the devil and his angels. So long as we are ignorant of their wiles, they have almost inconceivable advantage; many give heed to their suggestions while they suppose themselves to be following the dictates of their own wisdom. This is why, as we approach the close of time, when Satan is to work with greatest power to deceive and destroy, he spreads everywhere the belief that he does not exist. It is his policy to conceal himself and his manner of working.

There is nothing that the great deceiver fears so much as that we shall become acquainted with his devices. The better to disguise his real character and purposes, he has caused himself to be so represented as to excite no stronger emotion than ridicule or contempt. He is well pleased to be painted as a ludicrous or loathsome object, misshapen, half animal and half human. He is pleased to hear his name used in sport and mockery by those who think themselves intelligent and well informed.

It is because he has masked himself with consummate skill that the question is so widely asked: "Does such a being really exist?" It is an evidence of his success that theories giving the lie to the plainest testimony of the Scriptures are so generally received in the religious world. And it is because Satan can most readily control the minds of those who are unconscious of his influence, that the word of God gives us so many examples of his malignant work, unveiling before us his secret forces, and thus placing us on our guard against his assaults.

The power and malice of Satan and his host might justly alarm us were it not that we may find shelter and deliverance in the superior power of our Redeemer. We carefully secure our houses with bolts and locks to protect our property and our lives from evil men; but we seldom think of the evil angels who are constantly seeking access to us, and against whose attacks we have, in our own strength, no method of defense. If permitted, they can distract our minds, disorder and torment our bodies, destroy our possessions and our lives. Their only delight is in misery and destruction. Fearful is the condition of those who resist the divine claims and yield to Satan's temptations, until God gives them up to the control of evil spirits. But those who follow Christ are ever safe under His watchcare. Angels that excel in strength are sent from heaven to protect them. The wicked one cannot break through the guard which God has stationed about His people.

Four

—Snares of Satan—

The great controversy between Christ and Satan, that has been carried forward for nearly six thousand years, is soon to close; and the wicked one redoubles his efforts to defeat the work of Christ in man's behalf and to fasten souls in his snares. To hold the people in darkness and impenitence till the Saviour's mediation is ended, and there is no longer a sacrifice for sin, is the object which he seeks to accomplish.

When there is no special effort made to resist his power, when indifference prevails in the church and the world, Satan is not concerned; for he is in no danger of losing those whom he is leading captive at his will. But when the attention is called to eternal things, and souls are inquiring, "What must I do to be saved?" he is on the ground, seeking to match his power against the power of Christ and to counteract the influence of the Holy Spirit.

The Scriptures declare that upon one occasion, when the angels of God came to present themselves before the Lord, Satan came also among them (Job 1:6), not to bow before the Eternal King, but to further his own malicious designs against the righteous. With the same object he is in attendance when men assemble for the worship of God. Though hidden from sight, he is working with all diligence to control the minds of the worshipers. Like a skillful general he lays his plans beforehand. As he sees the messenger of God searching the Scriptures, he takes note of the subject to be presented to the people. Then he employs all his cunning and shrewdness so to control circumstances that the message may not reach those whom he is deceiving on that very point. The one who most needs the warning will be urged into some business transaction which requires his presence, or will by some other means be prevented from hearing the words that might prove to him a savor of life unto life.

Again, Satan sees the Lord's servants burdened because of the spiritual darkness that enshrouds the people. He hears their earnest prayers for divine grace and power to break the spell of indifference, carelessness, and indolence. Then with renewed zeal he plies his arts. He tempts men to the indulgence of appetite or to some other form of self-gratification, and thus benumbs their sensibilities so that they fail to hear the very things which they most need to learn.

Satan well knows that all whom he can lead to neglect prayer and the searching of the Scriptures, will be overcome by his attacks. Therefore he invents every possible device to engross the mind. There has ever been a class professing godliness, who, instead of following on to know the truth, make it their religion to seek some fault of character or error of faith in those with whom they do not agree. Such are Satan's right-hand helpers. Accusers of the brethren are not few, and they are always active when God is at work and His servants are rendering Him true homage. They will put a false coloring upon the words and acts of those who love and obey the truth. They will represent the most earnest, zealous, self-denying servants of Christ as deceived or deceivers. It is their work to misrepresent the motives of every true and noble deed, to circulate insinuations, and arouse suspicion in the minds of the inexperienced. In every conceivable manner they will seek to cause that which is pure and righteous to be regarded as foul and deceptive.

But none need be deceived concerning them. It may be readily seen whose children they are, whose example they follow, and whose work they do. "Ye shall know them by their fruits." Matthew 7:16. Their course resembles that of Satan, the envenomed slanderer, "the accuser of our brethren." Revelation 12:10.

The great deceiver has many agents ready to present any and every kind of error to ensnare souls—heresies prepared to suit the varied tastes and capacities of those whom he would ruin. It is his plan to bring into the church insincere, unregenerate elements that will encourage doubt and unbelief, and hinder all who desire to see the work of God advance and to advance with it. Many who have no real faith in God or in His word assent to some principles of truth and pass as Christians, and thus they are enabled to introduce their errors as Scriptural doctrines.

The position that it is of no consequence what men believe is one of Satan's most successful deceptions. He knows that the truth, received in the love of it, sanctifies the soul of the receiver; therefore he is constantly seeking to substitute false theories, fables, another gospel. From the beginning the servants of God have contended against false teachers, not merely as vicious men, but as inculcators of falsehoods that were fatal to the soul. Elijah, Jeremiah, Paul, firmly and fearlessly opposed those who were turning men from the word of God. That liberality which regards a correct religious faith as unimportant found no favor with these holy defenders of the truth.

The vague and fanciful interpretations of Scripture, and the many conflicting theories concerning religious faith, that are found in the Christian world are the work of our great adversary to confuse minds so that they shall not discern the truth. And the discord and division which exist among the churches of Christendom are in a great measure due to the prevailing custom of wresting the Scriptures to support a favorite theory. Instead of carefully studying God's word with humility of heart to obtain a knowledge of His will, many seek only to discover something odd or original.

In order to sustain erroneous doctrines or unchristian practices, some will seize upon passages of Scripture separated from the context, perhaps quoting half of a single verse as proving their point, when the remaining portion would show the meaning to be quite the opposite. With the cunning of the serpent they entrench themselves behind disconnected utterances construed to suit their carnal desires. Thus do many willfully pervert the word of God. Others, who have an active imagination, seize upon the figures and symbols of Holy Writ, interpret them to suit their fancy, with little regard to the testimony of Scripture as its own interpreter, and then they present their vagaries as the teachings of the Bible.

Whenever the study of the Scriptures is entered upon without a prayerful, humble, teachable spirit, the plainest and simplest as well as the most difficult passages will be wrested from their true meaning. The papal leaders select such portions of Scripture as best serve their purpose, interpret to suit themselves, and then present these to the people, while they deny them the privilege of studying the Bible and understanding its sacred truths for themselves. The whole Bible should be given to the people just as it reads. It would be better for them not to have Bible instruction at all than to have the teaching of the Scriptures thus grossly misrepresented.

The Bible was designed to be a guide to all who wish to become acquainted with the will of their Maker. God gave to men the sure word of prophecy; angels and even Christ Himself came to make known to Daniel and John the things that must shortly come to pass. Those important matters that concern our salvation were not left involved in mystery. They were not revealed in such a way as to perplex and mislead the honest seeker after truth. Said the Lord by the prophet Habakkuk: "Write the vision, and make it plain, … that he may run that readeth it." Habakkuk 2:2. The word of God is plain to all who study it with a prayerful heart. Every truly honest soul will come to the light of truth. "Light is sown for the righteous." Psalm 97:11. And no church can advance in holiness unless its members are earnestly seeking for truth as for hid treasure.

By the cry, Liberality, men are blinded to the devices of their adversary, while he is all the time working steadily for the accomplishment of his object. As he succeeds in supplanting the Bible by human speculations, the law of God is set aside, and the churches are under the bondage of sin while they claim to be free.

To many, scientific research has become a curse. God has permitted a flood of light to be poured upon the world in discoveries in science and art; but even the greatest minds, if not guided by the word of God in their research, become bewildered in their attempts to investigate the relations of science and revelation.

Human knowledge of both material and spiritual things is partial and imperfect; therefore many are unable to harmonize their views of science with Scripture statements. Many accept mere theories and speculations as scientific facts, and they think that God's word is to be tested by the teachings of "science falsely so called." 1 Timothy 6:20. The Creator and His works are beyond their comprehension; and because they cannot explain these by natural laws, Bible history is regarded as unreliable. Those who doubt the reliability of the records of the Old and New Testaments too often go a step further and doubt the existence of God and attribute infinite power to nature. Having let go their anchor, they are left to beat about upon the rocks of infidelity.

Thus many err from the faith and are seduced by the devil. Men have endeavored to be wiser than their Creator; human philosophy has attempted to search out and explain mysteries which will never be revealed through the eternal ages. If men would but search and understand what God has made known of Himself and His purposes, they would obtain such a view of the glory, majesty, and power of Jehovah that they would realize their own littleness and would be content with that which has been revealed for themselves and their children.

It is a masterpiece of Satan's deceptions to keep the minds of men searching and conjecturing in regard to that which God has not made known and which He does not intend that we shall understand. It was thus that Lucifer lost his place in heaven. He became dissatisfied because all the secrets of God's purposes were not confided to him, and he entirely disregarded that which was revealed concerning his own work in the lofty position assigned him. By arousing the same discontent in the angels under his command, he caused their fall. Now he seeks to imbue the minds of men with the same spirit and to lead them also to disregard the direct commands of God.

Those who are unwilling to accept the plain, cutting truths of the Bible are continually seeking for pleasing fables that will quiet the conscience. The less spiritual, self-denying, and humiliating the doctrines presented, the greater the favor with which they are received. These persons degrade the intellectual powers to serve their carnal desires. Too wise in their own conceit to search the Scriptures with contrition of soul and earnest prayer for divine guidance, they have no shield from delusion. Satan is ready to supply the heart's desire, and he palms off his deceptions in the place of truth. It was thus that the papacy gained its power over the minds of men; and by rejection of the truth because it involves a cross, Protestants are following the same path. All who neglect the word of God to study convenience and policy, that they may not be at variance with the world, will be left to receive damnable heresy for religious truth. Every conceivable form of error will be accepted by those who willfully reject the truth. He who looks with horror upon one deception will readily receive another. The apostle Paul, speaking of a class who "received not the love of the truth, that they might be saved," declares: "For this cause God shall send them strong delusion, that they should believe a lie: that they all might be damned who believed not the truth, but had pleasure in unrighteousness." 2 Thessalonians 2:10-12. With such a warning before us it behooves us to be on our guard as to what doctrines we receive.

Among the most successful agencies of the great deceiver are the delusive teachings and lying wonders of spiritualism. Disguised as an angel of light, he spreads his nets where least suspected. If men would but study the Book of God with earnest prayer that they might understand it, they would not be left in darkness to receive false doctrines. But as they reject the truth they fall a prey to deception.

Another dangerous error is the doctrine that denies the deity of Christ, claiming that He had no existence before His advent to this world. This theory is received with favor by a large class who profess to believe the Bible; yet it directly contradicts the plainest statements of our Saviour concerning His relationship with the Father, His divine character, and His pre-existence. It cannot be entertained without the most unwarranted wresting of the Scriptures. It not only lowers man's conceptions of the work of redemption, but undermines faith in the Bible as a revelation from God. While this renders it the more dangerous, it makes it also harder to meet. If men reject the testimony of the inspired Scriptures concerning the deity of Christ, it is in vain to argue the point with them; for no argument, however conclusive, could convince them. "The natural man receiveth not the things of the Spirit of God: for they are foolishness unto him: neither can he know them, because they are spiritually discerned." 1 Corinthians 2:14. None who hold this error can have a true conception of the character or the mission of Christ, or of the great plan of God for man's redemption.

Still another subtle and mischievous error is the fast-spreading belief that Satan has no existence as a personal being; that the name is used in Scripture merely to represent men's evil thoughts and desires.

The teaching so widely echoed from popular pulpits, that the second advent of Christ is His coming to each individual at death, is a device to divert the minds of men from His personal coming in the clouds of heaven. For years Satan has thus been saying, "Behold, He is in the secret chambers" (Matthew 24:23-26); and many souls have been lost by accepting this deception.

Again, worldly wisdom teaches that prayer is not essential. Men of science claim that there can be no real answer to prayer; that this would be a violation of law, a miracle, and that miracles have no existence. The universe, say they, is governed by fixed laws, and God Himself does nothing contrary to these laws. Thus they represent God as bound by His own laws—as if the operation of divine laws could exclude divine freedom. Such teaching is opposed to the testimony of the Scriptures. Were not miracles wrought by Christ and His apostles? The same compassionate Saviour lives today, and He is as willing to listen to the prayer of faith as when He walked visibly among men. The natural cooperates with the supernatural. It is a part of God's plan to grant us, in answer to the prayer of faith, that which He would not bestow did we not thus ask.

Innumerable are the erroneous doctrines and fanciful ideas that are obtaining among the churches of Christendom. It is impossible to estimate the evil results of removing one of the landmarks fixed by the word of God. Few who venture to do this stop with the rejection of a single truth. The majority continue to set aside one after another of the principles of truth, until they become actual infidels.

The errors of popular theology have driven many a soul to skepticism who might otherwise have been a believer in the Scriptures. It is impossible for him to accept doctrines which outrage his sense of justice, mercy, and benevolence; and since these are represented as the teaching of the Bible, he refuses to receive it as the word of God.

And this is the object which Satan seeks to accomplish. There is nothing that he desires more than to destroy confidence in God and in His word. Satan stands at the head of the great army of doubters, and he works to the utmost of his power to beguile souls into his ranks. It is becoming fashionable to doubt. There is a large class by whom the word of God is looked upon with distrust for the same reason as was its Author—because it reproves and condemns sin. Those who are unwilling to obey its requirements endeavor to overthrow its authority. They read the Bible, or listen to its teachings as presented from the sacred desk, merely to find fault with the Scriptures or with the sermon. Not a few become infidels in order to justify or excuse themselves in neglect of duty. Others adopt skeptical principles from pride and indolence. Too ease-loving to distinguish themselves by accomplishing anything worthy of honor, which requires effort and self-denial, they aim to secure a reputation for superior wisdom by criticizing the Bible. There is much which the finite mind, unenlightened by divine wisdom, is powerless to comprehend; and thus they find occasion to criticize. There are many who seem to feel that it is a virtue to stand on the side of unbelief, skepticism, and infidelity. But underneath an appearance of candor it will be found that such persons are actuated by self-confidence and pride. Many delight in finding something in the Scriptures to puzzle the minds of others. Some at first criticize and reason on the wrong side, from a mere love of controversy. They do not realize that they are thus entangling themselves in the snare of the fowler. But having openly expressed unbelief, they feel that they must maintain their position. Thus they unite with the ungodly and close to themselves the gates of Paradise.

God has given in His word sufficient evidence of its divine character. The great truths which concern our redemption are clearly presented. By the aid of the Holy Spirit, which is promised to all who seek it in sincerity, every man may understand these truths for himself. God has granted to men a strong foundation upon which to rest their faith.

Yet the finite minds of men are inadequate fully to comprehend the plans and purposes of the Infinite One. We can never by searching find out God. We must not attempt to lift with presumptuous hand the curtain behind which He veils His majesty. The apostle exclaims: "How unsearchable are His judgments, and His ways past finding out!" Romans 11:33. We can so far comprehend His dealings with us, and the motives by which He is actuated, that we may discern boundless love and mercy united to infinite power. Our Father in heaven orders everything in wisdom and righteousness, and we are not to be dissatisfied and distrustful, but to bow in reverent submission. He will reveal to us as much of His purposes as it is for our good to know, and beyond that we must trust the Hand that is omnipotent, the Heart that is full of love.

While God has given ample evidence for faith, He will never remove all excuse for unbelief. All who look for hooks to hang their doubts upon will find them. And those who refuse to accept and obey God's word until every objection has been removed, and there is no longer an opportunity for doubt, will never come to the light.

Distrust of God is the natural outgrowth of the unrenewed heart, which is at enmity with Him. But faith is inspired by the Holy Spirit, and it will flourish only as it is cherished. No man can become strong in faith without a determined effort. Unbelief strengthens as it is encouraged; and if men, instead of dwelling upon the evidences which God has given to sustain their faith, permit themselves to question and cavil, they will find their doubts constantly becoming more confirmed.

But those who doubt God's promises and distrust the assurance of His grace are dishonoring Him; and their influence, instead of drawing others to Christ, tends to repel them from Him. They are unproductive trees, that spread their dark branches far and wide, shutting away the sunlight from other plants, and causing them to droop and die under the chilling shadow. The lifework of these persons will appear as a never-ceasing witness against them. They are sowing seeds of doubt and skepticism that will yield an unfailing harvest.

There is but one course for those to pursue who honestly desire to be freed from doubts. Instead of questioning and caviling concerning that which they do not understand, let them give heed to the light which already shines upon them, and they will receive greater light. Let them do every duty which has been made plain to their understanding, and they will be enabled to understand and perform those of which they are now in doubt.

Satan can present a counterfeit so closely resembling the truth that it deceives those who are willing to be deceived, who desire to shun the self-denial and sacrifice demanded by the truth; but it is impossible for him to hold under his power one soul who honestly desires, at whatever cost, to know the truth. Christ is the truth and the "Light, which lighteth every man that cometh into the world." John 1:9. The Spirit of truth has been sent to guide men into all truth. And upon the authority of the Son of God it is declared: "Seek, and ye shall find." "If any man will do His will, he shall know of the doctrine." Matthew 7:7; John 7:17.

The followers of Christ know little of the plots which Satan and his hosts are forming against them. But He who sitteth in the heavens will overrule all these devices for the accomplishment of His deep designs. The Lord permits His people to be subjected to the fiery ordeal of temptation, not because He takes pleasure in their distress and affliction, but because this process is essential to their final victory. He could not, consistently with His own glory, shield them from temptation; for the very object of the trial is to prepare them to resist all the allurements of evil.

Neither wicked men nor devils can hinder the work of God, or shut out His presence from His people, if they will, with subdued, contrite hearts, confess and put away their sins, and in faith claim His promises. Every temptation, every opposing influence, whether open or secret, may be successfully resisted, "not by might, nor by power, but by My Spirit, saith the Lord of hosts." Zechariah 4:6.

"The eyes of the Lord are over the righteous, and His ears are open unto their prayers. ... And who is he that will harm you, if ye be followers of that which is good?" 1 Peter 3:12, 13. When Balaam, allured by the promise of rich rewards, practiced enchantments against Israel, and by sacrifices to the Lord sought to invoke a curse upon His people, the Spirit of God forbade the evil which he longed to pronounce, and Balaam was forced to exclaim: "How shall I curse, whom God hath not cursed? or how shall I defy, whom the Lord hath not defied?" "Let me die the death of the righteous, and let my last end be like his!" When sacrifice had again been offered, the ungodly prophet declared: "Behold, I have received commandment to bless: and He hath blessed; and I cannot reverse it. He hath not beheld iniquity in Jacob, neither hath He seen perverseness in Israel: the Lord his God is with him, and the shout of a King is among them." "Surely there is no enchantment against Jacob, neither is there any divination against Israel: according to this time it shall be said of Jacob and of Israel, What hath God wrought!" Yet a third time altars were erected, and again Balaam essayed to secure a curse. But from the unwilling lips of the prophet, the Spirit of God declared the prosperity of His chosen, and rebuked the folly and malice of their foes: "Blessed is he that blesseth thee, and cursed is he that curseth thee." Numbers 23:8, 10, 20, 21, 23; 24:9.

The people of Israel were at this time loyal to God; and so long as they continued in obedience to His law, no power in earth or hell could prevail against them. But the curse which Balaam had not been permitted to pronounce against God's people, he finally succeeded in bringing upon them by seducing them into sin. When they transgressed God's commandments, then they separated themselves from Him, and they were left to feel the power of the destroyer.

Satan is well aware that the weakest soul who abides in Christ is more than a match for the hosts of darkness, and that, should he reveal himself openly, he would be met and resisted. Therefore he seeks to draw away the soldiers of the cross from their strong fortification, while he lies in ambush with his forces, ready to destroy all who venture upon his ground. Only in humble reliance upon God, and obedience to all His commandments, can we be secure.

No man is safe for a day or an hour without prayer. Especially should we entreat the Lord for wisdom to understand His word. Here are revealed the wiles of the tempter and the means by which he may be successfully resisted. Satan is an expert in quoting Scripture, placing his own interpretation upon passages, by which he hopes to cause us to stumble. We should study the Bible with humility of heart, never losing sight of our dependence upon God. While we must constantly guard against the devices of Satan, we should pray in faith continually: "Lead us not into temptation."

Five

—Persecution in the First Centuries—

When Jesus revealed to His disciples the fate of Jerusalem and the scenes of the second advent, He foretold also the experience of His people from the time when He should be taken from them, to His return in power and glory for their deliverance. From Olivet the Saviour beheld the storms about to fall upon the apostolic church; and penetrating deeper into the future, His eye discerned the fierce, wasting tempests that were to beat upon His followers in the coming ages of darkness and persecution. In a few brief utterances of awful significance He foretold the portion which the rulers of this world would mete out to the church of God. Matthew 24:9, 21, 22. The followers of Christ must tread the same path of humiliation, reproach, and suffering which their Master trod. The enmity that burst forth against the world's Redeemer would be manifested against all who should believe on His name.

The history of the early church testified to the fulfillment of the Saviour's words. The powers of earth and hell arrayed themselves against Christ in the person of His followers. Paganism foresaw that should the gospel triumph, her temples and altars would be swept away; therefore she summoned her forces to destroy Christianity. The fires of persecution were kindled. Christians were stripped of their possessions and driven from their homes. They "endured a great fight of afflictions." Hebrews 10:32. They "had trial of cruel mockings and scourgings, yea, moreover of bonds and imprisonment." Hebrews 11:36. Great numbers sealed their testimony with their blood. Noble and slave, rich and poor, learned and ignorant, were alike slain without mercy.

These persecutions, beginning under Nero about the time of the martyrdom of Paul, continued with greater or less fury for centuries. Christians were falsely accused of the most dreadful crimes and declared to be the cause of great calamities—famine, pestilence, and earthquake. As they became the objects of popular hatred and suspicion, informers stood ready, for the sake of gain, to betray the innocent. They were condemned as rebels against the empire, as foes of religion, and pests to society. Great numbers were thrown to wild beasts or burned alive in the amphitheaters. Some were crucified; others were covered with the skins of wild animals and thrust into the arena to be torn by dogs. Their punishment was often made the chief entertainment at public fetes. Vast multitudes assembled to enjoy the sight and greeted their dying agonies with laughter and applause.

Wherever they sought refuge, the followers of Christ were hunted like beasts of prey. They were forced to seek concealment in desolate and solitary places. "Destitute, afflicted, tormented; (of whom the world was not worthy:) they wandered in deserts, and in mountains, and in dens and caves of the earth." Verses 37, 38. The catacombs afforded shelter for thousands. Beneath the hills outside the city of Rome, long galleries had been tunneled through earth and rock; the dark and intricate network of passages extended for miles beyond the city walls. In these underground retreats the followers of Christ buried their dead; and here also, when suspected and proscribed, they found a home. When the Life-giver shall awaken those who have fought the good fight, many a martyr for Christ's sake will come forth from those gloomy caverns.

Under the fiercest persecution these witnesses for Jesus kept their faith unsullied. Though deprived of every comfort, shut away from the light of the sun, making their home in the dark but friendly bosom of the earth, they uttered no complaint. With words of faith, patience, and hope they encouraged one another to endure privation and distress. The loss of every earthly blessing could not force them to renounce their belief in Christ. Trials and persecution were but steps bringing them nearer their rest and their reward.

Like God's servants of old, many were "tortured, not accepting deliverance; that they might obtain a better resurrection." Verse 35. These called to mind the words of their Master, that when persecuted for Christ's sake, they were to be exceeding glad, for great would be their reward in heaven; for so the prophets had been persecuted before them. They rejoiced that they were accounted worthy to suffer for the truth, and songs of triumph ascended from the midst of crackling flames. Looking upward by faith, they saw Christ and angels leaning over the battlements of heaven, gazing upon them with the deepest interest and regarding their steadfastness with approval. A voice came down to them from the throne of God: "Be thou faithful unto death, and I will give thee a crown of life." Revelation 2:10.

In vain were Satan's efforts to destroy the church of Christ by violence. The great controversy in which the disciples of Jesus yielded up their lives did not cease when these faithful standard-bearers fell at their post. By defeat they conquered. God's workmen were slain, but His work went steadily forward. The gospel continued to spread and the number of its adherents to increase. It penetrated into regions that were inaccessible even to the eagles of Rome. Said a Christian, expostulating with the heathen rulers who were urging forward the persecution: You may "kill us, torture us, condemn us. ... Your injustice is the proof that we are innocent. ... Nor does your cruelty ... avail you." It was but a stronger invitation to bring others to their persuasion. "The oftener we are mown down by you, the more in number we grow; the blood of Christians is seed."—Tertullian, *Apology*, paragraph 50.

Thousands were imprisoned and slain, but others sprang up to fill their places. And those who were martyred for their faith were secured to Christ and accounted of Him as conquerors. They had fought the good fight, and they were to receive the crown of glory when Christ should come. The sufferings which they endured brought Christians nearer to one another and to their Redeemer. Their living example and dying testimony were a constant witness for the truth; and where least expected, the subjects of Satan were leaving his service and enlisting under the banner of Christ.

Satan therefore laid his plans to war more successfully against the government of God by planting his banner in the Christian church. If the followers of Christ could be deceived and led to displease God, then their strength, fortitude, and firmness would fail, and they would fall an easy prey.

The great adversary now endeavored to gain by artifice what he had failed to secure by force. Persecution ceased, and in its stead were substituted the dangerous allurements of temporal prosperity and worldly honor. Idolaters were led to receive a part of the Christian faith, while they rejected other essential truths. They professed to accept Jesus as the Son of God and to believe in His death and resurrection, but they had no conviction of sin and felt no need of repentance or of a change of heart. With some concessions on their part they proposed that Christians should make concessions, that all might unite on the platform of belief in Christ.

Now the church was in fearful peril. Prison, torture, fire, and sword were blessings in comparison with this. Some of the Christians stood firm, declaring that they could make no compromise. Others were in favor of yielding or modifying some features of their faith and uniting with those who had accepted a part of Christianity, urging that this might be the means of their full conversion. That was a time of deep anguish to the faithful followers of Christ. Under a cloak of pretended Christianity, Satan was insinuating himself into the church, to corrupt their faith and turn their minds from the word of truth.

Most of the Christians at last consented to lower their standard, and a union was formed between Christianity and paganism. Although the worshipers of idols professed to be converted, and united with the church, they still clung to their idolatry, only changing the objects of their worship to images of Jesus, and even of Mary and the saints. The foul leaven of idolatry, thus brought into the church, continued its baleful work. Unsound doctrines, superstitious rites, and idolatrous ceremonies were incorporated into her faith and worship. As the followers of Christ united with idolaters, the Christian religion became corrupted, and the church lost her purity and power. There were some, however, who were not misled by these delusions. They still maintained their fidelity to the Author of truth and worshiped God alone.

There have ever been two classes among those who profess to be followers of Christ. While one class study the Saviour's life and earnestly seek to correct their defects and conform to the Pattern, the other class shun the plain, practical truths which expose their errors. Even in her best estate the church was not composed wholly of the true, pure, and sincere. Our Saviour taught that those who willfully indulge in sin are not to be received into the church; yet He connected with Himself men who were faulty in character, and granted them the benefits of His teachings and example, that they might have an opportunity to see their errors and correct them. Among the twelve apostles was a traitor. Judas was accepted, not because of his defects of character, but notwithstanding them. He was connected with the disciples, that, through the instruction and example of Christ, he might learn what constitutes Christian character, and thus be led to see his errors, to repent, and, by the aid of divine grace, to purify his soul "in obeying the truth." But Judas did not walk in the light so graciously permitted to shine upon him. By indulgence in sin he invited the temptations of Satan. His evil traits of character became predominant. He yielded his mind to the control of the powers of darkness, he became angry when his faults were reproved, and thus he was led to commit the fearful crime of betraying his Master. So do all who cherish evil under a profession of godliness hate those who disturb their peace by condemning their course of sin. When a favorable opportunity is presented, they will, like Judas, betray those who for their good have sought to reprove them.

The apostles encountered those in the church who professed godliness while they were secretly cherishing iniquity. Ananias and Sapphira acted the part of deceivers, pretending to make an entire sacrifice for God, when they were covetously withholding a portion for themselves. The Spirit of truth revealed to the apostles the real character of these pretenders, and the judgments of God rid the church of this foul blot upon its purity. This signal evidence of the discerning Spirit of Christ in the church was a terror to hypocrites and evildoers. They could not long remain in connection with those who were, in habit and disposition, constant representatives of Christ; and as trials and persecution came upon His followers, those only who were willing to forsake all for the truth's sake desired to become His disciples. Thus, as long as persecution continued, the church remained comparatively pure. But as it ceased, converts were added who were less sincere and devoted, and the way was open for Satan to obtain a foothold.

But there is no union between the Prince of light and the prince of darkness, and there can be no union between their followers. When Christians consented to unite with those who were but half converted from paganism, they entered upon a path which led further and further from the truth. Satan exulted that he had succeeded in deceiving so large a number of the followers of Christ. He then brought his power to bear more fully upon these, and inspired them to persecute those who remained true to God. None understood so well how to oppose the true Christian faith as did those who had once been its defenders; and these apostate Christians, uniting with their half-pagan companions, directed their warfare against the most essential features of the doctrines of Christ.

It required a desperate struggle for those who would be faithful to stand firm against the deceptions and abominations which were disguised in sacerdotal garments and introduced into the church. The Bible was not accepted as the standard of faith. The doctrine of religious freedom was termed heresy, and its upholders were hated and proscribed.

After a long and severe conflict, the faithful few decided to dissolve all union with the apostate church if she still refused to free herself from falsehood and idolatry. They saw that separation was an absolute necessity if they would obey the word of God. They dared not tolerate errors fatal to their own souls, and set an example which would imperil the faith of their children and children's children. To secure peace and unity they were ready to make any concession consistent with fidelity to God; but they felt that even peace would be too dearly purchased at the sacrifice of principle. If unity could be secured only by the compromise of truth and righteousness, then let there be difference, and even war.

Well would it be for the church and the world if the principles that actuated those steadfast souls were revived in the hearts of God's professed people. There is an alarming indifference in regard to the doctrines which are the pillars of the Christian faith. The opinion is gaining ground, that, after all, these are not of vital importance. This degeneracy is strengthening the hands of the agents of Satan, so that false theories and fatal delusions which the faithful in ages past imperiled their lives to resist and expose, are now regarded with favor by thousands who claim to be followers of Christ.

The early Christians were indeed a peculiar people. Their blameless deportment and unswerving faith were a continual reproof that disturbed the sinner's peace. Though few in numbers, without wealth, position, or honorary titles, they were a terror to evildoers wherever their character and doctrines were known. Therefore they were hated by the wicked, even as Abel was hated by the ungodly Cain. For the same reason that Cain slew Abel, did those who sought to throw off the restraint of the Holy Spirit, put to death God's people. It was for the same reason that the Jews rejected and crucified the Saviour—because the purity and holiness of His character was a constant rebuke to their selfishness and corruption. From the days of Christ until now His faithful disciples have excited the hatred and opposition of those who love and follow the ways of sin.

How, then, can the gospel be called a message of peace? When Isaiah foretold the birth of the Messiah, he ascribed to Him the title, "Prince of Peace." When angels announced to the shepherds that Christ was born, they sang above the plains of Bethlehem: "Glory to God in the highest, and on earth peace, good will toward men." Luke 2:14. There is a seeming contradiction between these prophetic declarations and the words of Christ: "I came not to send peace, but a sword." Matthew 10:34. But, rightly understood, the two are in perfect harmony. The gospel is a message of peace. Christianity is a system which, received and obeyed, would spread peace, harmony, and happiness throughout the earth. The religion of Christ will unite in close brotherhood all who accept its teachings. It was the mission of Jesus to reconcile men to God, and thus to one another. But the world at large are under the control of Satan, Christ's bitterest foe. The gospel presents to them principles of life which are wholly at variance with their habits and desires, and they rise in rebellion against it. They hate the purity which reveals and condemns their sins, and they persecute and destroy those who would urge upon them its just and holy claims. It is in this sense—because the exalted truths it brings occasion hatred and strife—that the gospel is called a sword.

The mysterious providence which permits the righteous to suffer persecution at the hand of the wicked has been a cause of great perplexity to many who are weak in faith. Some are even ready to cast away their confidence in God because He suffers the basest of men to prosper, while the best and purest are afflicted and tormented by their cruel power. How, it is asked, can One who is just and merciful, and who is also infinite in power, tolerate such injustice and oppression? This is a question with which we have nothing to do. God has given us sufficient evidence of His love, and we are not to doubt His goodness because we cannot understand the workings of His providence. Said the Saviour to His disciples, foreseeing the doubts that would press upon their souls in days of trial and darkness: "Remember the word that I said unto you, The servant is not greater than his lord. If they have persecuted Me, they will also persecute you." John 15:20. Jesus suffered for us more than any of His followers can be made to suffer through the cruelty of wicked men. Those who are called to endure torture and martyrdom are but following in the steps of God's dear Son.

"The Lord is not slack concerning His promise." 2 Peter 3:9. He does not forget or neglect His children; but He permits the wicked to reveal their true character, that none who desire to do His will may be deceived concerning them. Again, the righteous are placed in the furnace of affliction, that they themselves may be purified; that their example may convince others of the reality of faith and godliness; and also that their consistent course may condemn the ungodly and unbelieving.

God permits the wicked to prosper and to reveal their enmity against Him, that when they shall have filled up the measure of their iniquity all may see His justice and mercy in their utter destruction. The day of His vengeance hastens, when all who have transgressed His law and oppressed His people will meet the just recompense of their deeds; when every act of cruelty or injustice toward God's faithful ones will be punished as though done to Christ Himself.

There is another and more important question that should engage the attention of the churches of today. The apostle Paul declares that "all that will live godly in Christ Jesus shall suffer persecution." 2 Timothy 3:12. Why is it, then, that persecution seems in a great degree to slumber? The only reason is that the church has conformed to the world's standard and therefore awakens no opposition. The religion which is current in our day is not of the pure and holy character that marked the Christian faith in the days of Christ and His apostles. It is only because of the spirit of compromise with sin, because the great truths of the word of God are so indifferently regarded, because there is so little vital godliness in the church, that Christianity is apparently so popular with the world. Let there be a revival of the faith and power of the early church, and the spirit of persecution will be revived, and the fires of persecution will be rekindled.

Six

—An Era of Spiritual Darkness—

The apostle Paul, in his second letter to the Thessalonians, foretold the great apostasy which would result in the establishment of the papal power. He declared that the day of Christ should not come, "except there come a falling away first, and that man of sin be revealed, the son of perdition; who opposeth and exalteth himself above all that is called God, or that is worshiped; so that he as God sitteth in the temple of God, showing himself that he is God." And furthermore, the apostle warns his brethren that "the mystery of iniquity doth already work." 2 Thessalonians 2:3, 4, 7. Even at that early date he saw, creeping into the church, errors that would prepare the way for the development of the papacy.

Little by little, at first in stealth and silence, and then more openly as it increased in strength and gained control of the minds of men, "the mystery of iniquity" carried forward its deceptive and blasphemous work. Almost imperceptibly the customs of heathenism found their way into the Christian church. The spirit of compromise and conformity was restrained for a time by the fierce persecutions which the church endured under paganism. But as persecution ceased, and Christianity entered the courts and palaces of kings, she laid aside the humble simplicity of Christ and His apostles for the pomp and pride of pagan priests and rulers; and in place of the requirements of God, she substituted human theories and traditions. The nominal conversion of Constantine, in the early part of the fourth century, caused great rejoicing; and the world, cloaked with a form of righteousness, walked into the church. Now the work of corruption rapidly progressed. Paganism, while appearing to be vanquished, became the conqueror. Her spirit controlled the church. Her doctrines, ceremonies, and superstitions were incorporated into the faith and worship of the professed followers of Christ.

This compromise between paganism and Christianity resulted in the development of "the man of sin" foretold in prophecy as opposing and exalting himself above God. That gigantic system of false religion is a masterpiece of Satan's power—a monument of his efforts to seat himself upon the throne to rule the earth according to his will.

Satan once endeavored to form a compromise with Christ. He came to the Son of God in the wilderness of temptation, and showing Him all the kingdoms of the world and the glory of them, offered to give all into His hands if He would but acknowledge the supremacy of the prince of darkness. Christ rebuked the presumptuous tempter and forced him to depart. But Satan meets with greater success in presenting the same temptations to man. To secure worldly gains and honors, the church was led to seek the favor and support of the great men of earth; and having thus rejected Christ, she was induced to yield allegiance to the representative of Satan—the bishop of Rome.

It is one of the leading doctrines of Romanism that the pope is the visible head of the universal church of Christ, invested with supreme authority over bishops and pastors in all parts of the world. More than this, the pope has been given the very titles of Deity. He has been styled "Lord God the Pope", and has been declared infallible. He demands the homage of all men. The same claim urged by Satan in the wilderness of temptation is still urged by him through the Church of Rome, and vast numbers are ready to yield him homage.

But those who fear and reverence God meet this heaven-daring assumption as Christ met the solicitations of the wily foe: "Thou shalt worship the Lord thy God, and Him only shalt thou serve." Luke 4:8. God has never given a hint in His word that He has appointed any man to be the head of the church. The doctrine of papal supremacy is directly opposed to the teachings of the Scriptures. The pope can have no power over Christ's church except by usurpation.

Romanists have persisted in bringing against Protestants the charge of heresy and willful separation from the true church. But these accusations apply rather to themselves. They are the ones who laid down the banner of Christ and departed from "the faith which was once delivered unto the saints." Jude 3.

Satan well knew that the Holy Scriptures would enable men to discern his deceptions and withstand his power. It was by the word that even the Saviour of the world had resisted his attacks. At every assault,

Christ presented the shield of eternal truth, saying, "It is written." To every suggestion of the adversary, He opposed the wisdom and power of the word. In order for Satan to maintain his sway over men, and establish the authority of the papal usurper, he must keep them in ignorance of the Scriptures. The Bible would exalt God and place finite men in their true position; therefore its sacred truths must be concealed and suppressed. This logic was adopted by the Roman Church. For hundreds of years the circulation of the Bible was prohibited. The people were forbidden to read it or to have it in their houses, and unprincipled priests and prelates interpreted its teachings to sustain their pretensions. Thus the pope came to be almost universally acknowledged as the vicegerent of God on earth, endowed with authority over church and state.

The detector of error having been removed, Satan worked according to his will. Prophecy had declared that the papacy was to "think to change times and laws." Daniel 7:25. This work it was not slow to attempt. To afford converts from heathenism a substitute for the worship of idols, and thus to promote their nominal acceptance of Christianity, the adoration of images and relics was gradually introduced into the Christian worship. The decree of a general council finally established this system of idolatry. To complete the sacrilegious work, Rome presumed to expunge from the law of God the second commandment, forbidding image worship, and to divide the tenth commandment, in order to preserve the number.

The spirit of concession to paganism opened the way for a still further disregard of Heaven's authority. Satan, working through unconsecrated leaders of the church, tampered with the fourth commandment also, and essayed to set aside the ancient Sabbath, the day which God had blessed and sanctified (Genesis 2:2,3), and in its stead to exalt the festival observed by the heathen as "the venerable day of the sun." This change was not at first attempted openly. In the first centuries the true Sabbath had been kept by all Christians. They were jealous for the honor of God, and, believing that His law is immutable, they zealously guarded the sacredness of its precepts. But with great subtlety Satan worked through his agents to bring about his object. That the attention of the people might be called to the Sunday, it was made a festival in honor of the resurrection of Christ. Religious services were held upon it; yet it was regarded as a day of recreation, the Sabbath being still sacredly observed.

To prepare the way for the work which he designed to accomplish, Satan had led the Jews, before the advent of Christ, to load down the Sabbath with the most rigorous exactions, making its observance a burden. Now, taking advantage of the false light in which he had thus caused it to be regarded, he cast contempt upon it as a Jewish institution. While Christians generally continued to observe the Sunday as a joyous festival, he led them, in order to show their hatred of Judaism, to make the Sabbath a fast, a day of sadness and gloom.

In the early part of the fourth century the emperor Constantine issued a decree making Sunday a public festival throughout the Roman Empire. The day of the sun was reverenced by his pagan subjects and was honored by Christians; it was the emperor's policy to unite the conflicting interests of heathenism and Christianity. He was urged to do this by the bishops of the church, who, inspired by ambition and thirst for power, perceived that if the same day was observed by both Christians and heathen, it would promote the nominal acceptance of Christianity by pagans and thus advance the power and glory of the church. But while many God-fearing Christians were gradually led to regard Sunday as possessing a degree of sacredness, they still held the true Sabbath as the holy of the Lord and observed it in obedience to the fourth commandment.

The archdeceiver had not completed his work. He was resolved to gather the Christian world under his banner and to exercise his power through his vicegerent, the proud pontiff who claimed to be the representative of Christ. Through half-converted pagans, ambitious prelates, and world-loving churchmen he accomplished his purpose. Vast councils were held from time to time, in which the dignitaries of the church were convened from all the world. In nearly every council the Sabbath which God had instituted was pressed down a little lower, while the Sunday was correspondingly exalted. Thus the pagan festival came finally to be honored as a divine institution, while the Bible Sabbath was pronounced a relic of Judaism, and its observers were declared to be accursed.

The great apostate had succeeded in exalting himself "above all that is called God, or that is worshiped." 2 Thessalonians 2:4. He had dared to change the only precept of the divine law that unmistakably points all mankind to the true and living God. In the fourth commandment, God is revealed as the Creator of the heavens and the earth, and is thereby distinguished from all false gods. It was as a memorial of the work of creation that the seventh day was sanctified as a rest day for man. It was designed to keep the living God ever before the minds of men as the source of being and the object of reverence and worship. Satan strives to turn men from their allegiance to God, and from rendering obedience to His law; therefore he directs his efforts especially against that commandment which points to God as the Creator.

Protestants now urge that the resurrection of Christ on Sunday made it the Christian Sabbath. But Scripture evidence is lacking. No such honor was given to the day by Christ or His apostles. The observance of Sunday as a Christian institution had its origin in that "mystery of lawlessness" (2 Thessalonians 2:7, R.V.) which, even in Paul's day, had begun its work. Where and when did the Lord adopt this child of the papacy? What valid reason can be given for a change which the Scriptures do not sanction?

In the sixth century the papacy had become firmly established. Its seat of power was fixed in the imperial city, and the bishop of Rome was declared to be the head over the entire church. Paganism had given place to the papacy. The dragon had given to the beast "his power, and his seat, and great authority." Revelation 13:2. And now began the 1,260 years of papal oppression foretold in the prophecies of Daniel and the Revelation. Daniel 7:25; Revelation 13:5-7. Christians were forced to choose either to yield their integrity and accept the papal ceremonies and worship, or to wear away their lives in dungeons or suffer death by the rack, the fagot, or the headsman's ax. Now were fulfilled the words of Jesus: "Ye shall be betrayed both by parents, and brethren, and kinsfolks, and friends; and some of you shall they cause to be put to death. And ye shall be hated of all men for My name's sake." Luke 21:16, 17. Persecution opened upon the faithful with greater fury than ever before, and the world became a vast battlefield. For hundreds of years the church of Christ found refuge in seclusion and obscurity. Thus says the prophet: "The woman fled into the wilderness, where she hath a place prepared of God, that they should feed her there a thousand two hundred and threescore days." Revelation 12:6.

The accession of the Roman Church to power marked the beginning of the Dark Ages. As her power increased, the darkness deepened. Faith was transferred from Christ, the true foundation, to the pope of Rome. Instead of trusting in the Son of God for forgiveness of sins and for eternal salvation, the people looked to the pope, and to the priests and prelates to whom he delegated authority. They were taught that the pope was their earthly mediator and that none could approach God except through him; and, further, that he stood in the place of God to them and was therefore to be implicitly obeyed. A deviation from his requirements was sufficient cause for the severest punishment to be visited upon the bodies and souls of the offenders. Thus the minds of the people were turned away from God to fallible, erring, and cruel men, nay, more, to the prince of darkness himself, who exercised his power through them. Sin was disguised in a garb of sanctity. When the Scriptures are suppressed, and man comes to regard himself as supreme, we need look only for fraud, deception, and debasing iniquity. With the elevation of human laws and traditions was manifest the corruption that ever results from setting aside the law of God.

Those were days of peril for the church of Christ. The faithful standard-bearers were few indeed. Though the truth was not left without witnesses, yet at times it seemed that error and superstition would wholly prevail, and true religion would be banished from the earth. The gospel was lost sight of, but the forms of religion were multiplied, and the people were burdened with rigorous exactions.

They were taught not only to look to the pope as their mediator, but to trust to works of their own to atone for sin. Long pilgrimages, acts of penance, the worship of relics, the erection of churches, shrines, and altars, the payment of large sums to the church—these and many similar acts were enjoined to appease the wrath of God or to secure His favor; as if God were like men, to be angered at trifles, or pacified by gifts or acts of penance!

Notwithstanding that vice prevailed, even among the leaders of the Roman Church, her influence seemed steadily to increase. About the close of the eighth century, papists put forth the claim that in the first ages of the church the bishops of Rome had possessed the same spiritual power which they now assumed. To establish this claim, some means must be employed to give it a show of authority; and this was readily suggested by the father of lies. Ancient writings were forged by monks. Decrees of councils before unheard of were discovered, establishing the universal supremacy of the pope from the earliest times. And a church that had rejected the truth greedily accepted these deceptions.

The few faithful builders upon the true foundation. (1 Corinthians 3:10, 11) were perplexed and hindered as the rubbish of false doctrine obstructed the work. Like the builders upon the wall of Jerusalem in Nehemiah's day, some were ready to say: "The strength of the bearers of burdens is decayed, and there is much rubbish; so that we are not able to build." Nehemiah 4:10. Wearied with the constant struggle against perse–cution, fraud, iniquity, and every other obstacle that Satan could devise to hinder their progress, some who had been faithful builders became disheartened; and for the sake of peace and security for their property and their lives, they turned away from the true foundation. Others, undaunted by the opposition of their enemies, fearlessly declared: "Be not ye afraid of them: remember the Lord, which is great and terrible" (verse 14); and they proceeded with the work, everyone with his sword girded by his side. Ephesians 6:17.

The same spirit of hatred and opposition to the truth has inspired the enemies of God in every age, and the same vigilance and fidelity have been required in His servants. The words of Christ to the first disciples are applicable to His followers to the close of time: "What I say unto you I say unto all, Watch." Mark 13:37.

The darkness seemed to grow more dense. Image worship became more general. Candles were burned before images, and prayers were offered to them. The most absurd and superstitious customs prevailed. The minds of men were so completely controlled by superstition that reason itself seemed to have lost its sway. While priests and bishops were themselves pleasure-loving, sensual, and corrupt, it could only be expected that the people who looked to them for guidance would be sunken in ignorance and vice.

Another step in papal assumption was taken, when, in the eleventh century, Pope Gregory VII proclaimed the perfection of the Roman Church. Among the propositions which he put forth was one declaring that the church had never erred, nor would it ever err, according to the Scriptures. But the Scripture proofs did not accompany the assertion. The proud pontiff also claimed the power to depose emperors, and declared that no sentence which he pronounced could be reversed by anyone, but that it was his prerogative to reverse the decisions of all others.

A striking illustration of the tyrannical character of this advocate of infallibility was given in his treatment of the German emperor, Henry IV. For presuming to disregard the pope's authority, this monarch was declared to be excommunicated and dethroned. Terrified by the desertion and threats of his own princes, who were encouraged in rebellion against him by the papal mandate, Henry felt the necessity of making his peace with Rome. In company with his wife and a faithful servant he crossed the Alps in midwinter, that he might humble himself before the pope. Upon reaching the castle whither Gregory had withdrawn, he was conducted, without his guards, into an outer court, and there, in the severe cold of winter, with uncovered head and naked feet, and in a miserable dress, he awaited the pope's permission to come into his presence. Not until he had continued three days fasting and making confession, did the pontiff condescend to grant him pardon. Even then it was only upon condition that the emperor should await the sanction of the pope before resuming the insignia or exercising the power of royalty. And Gregory, elated with his triumph, boasted that it was his duty to pull down the pride of kings.

How striking the contrast between the overbearing pride of this haughty pontiff and the meekness and gentleness of Christ, who represents Himself as pleading at the door of the heart for admittance, that He may come in to bring pardon and peace, and who taught His disciples: "Whosoever will be chief among you, let him be your servant." Matthew 20:27.

The advancing centuries witnessed a constant increase of error in the doctrines put forth from Rome. Even before the establishment of the papacy the teachings of heathen philosophers had received attention and exerted an influence in the church. Many who professed conversion still clung to the tenets of their pagan philosophy, and not only continued its study themselves, but urged it upon others as a means of extending their influence among the heathen. Serious errors were thus introduced into the Christian faith. Prominent among these was the belief in man's natural immortality and his consciousness in death. This doctrine laid the foundation upon which Rome established the invocation of saints and the adoration of the Virgin Mary. From this sprang also the heresy of eternal torment for the finally impenitent, which was early incorporated into the papal faith.

Then the way was prepared for the introduction of still another invention of paganism, which Rome named purgatory, and employed to terrify the credulous and superstitious multitudes. By this heresy is affirmed the existence of a place of torment, in which the souls of such as have not merited eternal damnation are to suffer punishment for their sins, and from which, when freed from impurity, they are admitted to heaven.

Still another fabrication was needed to enable Rome to profit by the fears and the vices of her adherents. This was supplied by the doctrine of indulgences. Full remission of sins, past, present, and future, and release from all the pains and penalties incurred, were promised to all who would enlist in the pontiff's wars to extend his temporal dominion, to punish his enemies, or to exterminate those who dared deny his spiritual supremacy. The people were also taught that by the payment of money to the church they might free themselves from sin, and also release the souls of their deceased friends who were confined in the tormenting flames. By such means did Rome fill her coffers and sustain the magnificence, luxury, and vice of the pretended representatives of Him who had not where to lay His head.

The Scriptural ordinance of the Lord's Supper had been supplanted by the idolatrous sacrifice of the mass. Papal priests pretended, by their senseless mummery, to convert the simple bread and wine into the actual "body and blood of Christ."—Cardinal Wiseman, *The Real Presence of the Body and Blood of Our Lord Jesus Christ in the Blessed Eucharist, Proved From Scripture*, lecture 8, sec. 3, par. 26. With blasphemous presumption, they openly claimed the power of creating God, the Creator of all things. Christians were required, on pain of death, to avow their faith in this horrible, Heaven-insulting heresy. Multitudes who refused were given to the flames.

In the thirteenth century was established that most terrible of all the engines of the papacy—the Inquisition. The prince of darkness wrought with the leaders of the papal hierarchy. In their secret councils Satan and his angels controlled the minds of evil men, while unseen in the midst stood an angel of God, taking the fearful record of their iniquitous decrees and writing the history of deeds too horrible to appear to human eyes. "Babylon the great" was "drunken with the blood of the saints." The mangled forms of millions of martyrs cried to God for vengeance upon that apostate power.

Popery had become the world's despot. Kings and emperors bowed to the decrees of the Roman pontiff. The destinies of men, both for time and for eternity, seemed under his control. For hundreds of years the doctrines of Rome had been extensively and implicitly received, its rites reverently performed, its festivals generally observed. Its clergy were honored and liberally sustained. Never since has the Roman Church attained to greater dignity, magnificence, or power.

But "the noon of the papacy was the midnight of the world."—J. A. Wylie, *The History of Protestantism*, b. 1, ch. 4. The Holy Scriptures were almost unknown, not only to the people, but to the priests. Like the Pharisees of old, the papal leaders hated the light which would reveal their sins. God's law, the standard of righteousness, having been removed, they exercised power without limit, and practiced vice without restraint. Fraud, avarice, and profligacy prevailed. Men shrank from no crime by which they could gain wealth or position. The palaces of popes and prelates were scenes of the vilest debauchery. Some of the reigning pontiffs were guilty of crimes so revolting that secular rulers endeavored to depose these dignitaries of the church as monsters too vile to be tolerated. For centuries Europe had made no progress in learning, arts, or civilization. A moral and intellectual paralysis had fallen upon Christendom.

The condition of the world under the Romish power presented a fearful and striking fulfillment of the words of the prophet Hosea: "My people are destroyed for lack of knowledge: because thou hast rejected knowledge, I will also reject thee: … seeing thou hast forgotten the law of thy God, I will also forget thy children." "There is no truth, nor mercy, nor knowledge of God in the land. By swearing, and lying, and killing, and stealing, and committing adultery, they break out, and blood toucheth blood." Hosea 4:6, 1, 2. Such were the results of banishing the word of God.

Seven

—The First Great Deception—

With the earliest history of man, Satan began his efforts to deceive our race. He who had incited rebellion in heaven desired to bring the inhabitants of the earth to unite with him in his warfare against the government of God. Adam and Eve had been perfectly happy in obedience to the law of God, and this fact was a constant testimony against the claim which Satan had urged in heaven, that God's law was oppressive and opposed to the good of His creatures. And furthermore, Satan's envy was excited as he looked upon the beautiful home prepared for the sinless pair. He determined to cause their fall, that, having separated them from God and brought them under his own power, he might gain possession of the earth and here establish his kingdom in opposition to the Most High.

Had Satan revealed himself in his real character, he would have been repulsed at once, for Adam and Eve had been warned against this dangerous foe; but he worked in the dark, concealing his purpose, that he might more effectually accomplish his object. Employing as his medium the serpent, then a creature of fascinating appearance, he addressed himself to Eve: "Hath God said, Ye shall not eat of every tree of the garden?" Genesis 3:1. Had Eve refrained from entering into argument with the tempter, she would have been safe; but she ventured to parley with him and fell a victim to his wiles. It is thus that many are still overcome. They doubt and argue concerning the requirements of God; and instead of obeying the divine commands, they accept human theories, which but disguise the devices of Satan.

"The woman said unto the serpent, We may eat of the fruit of the trees of the garden: but of the fruit of the tree which is in the midst of the garden, God hath said, Ye shall not eat of it, neither shall ye touch it, lest ye die. And the serpent said unto the woman, Ye shall not surely die: for God doth know that in the day ye eat thereof, then your eyes shall be opened, and ye shall be as gods, knowing good and evil." Verses 2-5. He declared that they would become like God, possessing greater wisdom than before and being capable of a higher state of existence. Eve yielded to temptation; and through her influence, Adam was led into sin. They accepted the words of the serpent, that God did not mean what He said; they distrusted their Creator and imagined that He was restricting their liberty and that they might obtain great wisdom and exaltation by transgressing His law.

But what did Adam, after his sin, find to be the meaning of the words, "In the day that thou eatest thereof thou shalt surely die"? Did he find them to mean, as Satan had led him to believe, that he was to be ushered into a more exalted state of existence? Then indeed there was great good to be gained by transgression, and Satan was proved to be a benefactor of the race. But Adam did not find this to be the meaning of the divine sentence. God declared that as a penalty for his sin, man should return to the ground whence he was taken: "Dust thou art, and unto dust shalt thou return." Verse 19. The words of Satan, "Your eyes shall be opened," proved to be true in this sense only: After Adam and Eve had disobeyed God, their eyes were opened to discern their folly; they did know evil, and they tasted the bitter fruit of transgression.

In the midst of Eden grew the tree of life, whose fruit had the power of perpetuating life. Had Adam remained obedient to God, he would have continued to enjoy free access to this tree and would have lived forever. But when he sinned he was cut off from partaking of the tree of life, and he became subject to death. The divine sentence, "Dust thou art, and unto dust shalt thou return," points to the utter extinction of life.

Immortality, promised to man on condition of obedience, had been forfeited by transgression. Adam could not transmit to his posterity that which he did not possess; and there could have been no hope for the fallen race had not God, by the sacrifice of His Son, brought immortality within their reach. While "death passed upon all men, for that all have sinned," Christ "hath brought life and immortality to light through the gospel." Romans 5:12; 2 Timothy 1:10. And only through Christ can immortality be obtained. Said Jesus: "He that believeth on the Son hath everlasting life: and he that believeth not the Son shall not see life." John 3:36. Every man may come into possession of this priceless blessing if he will comply with the conditions. All "who by patient continuance in well-doing seek for glory and honor and immortality," will receive "eternal life." Romans 2:7.

The only one who promised Adam life in disobedience was the great deceiver. And the declaration of the serpent to Eve in Eden—"Ye shall not surely die"—was the first sermon ever preached upon the immortality of the soul. Yet this declaration, resting solely upon the authority of Satan, is echoed from the pulpits of Christendom and is received by the majority of mankind as readily as it was received by our first parents. The divine sentence, "The soul that sinneth, it shall die" (Ezekiel 18:20), is made to mean: The soul that sinneth, it shall not die, but live eternally. We cannot but wonder at the strange infatuation which renders men so credulous concerning the words of Satan and so unbelieving in regard to the words of God.

Had man after his fall been allowed free access to the tree of life, he would have lived forever, and thus sin would have been immortalized. But cherubim and a flaming sword kept "the way of the tree of life" (Genesis 3:24), and not one of the family of Adam has been permitted to pass that barrier and partake of the life-giving fruit. Therefore there is not an immortal sinner.

But after the Fall, Satan bade his angels make a special effort to inculcate the belief in man's natural immortality; and having induced the people to receive this error, they were to lead them on to conclude that the sinner would live in eternal misery. Now the prince of darkness, working through his agents, represents God as a revengeful tyrant, declaring that He plunges into hell all those who do not please Him, and causes them ever to feel His wrath; and that while they suffer unutterable anguish and writhe in the eternal flames, their Creator looks down upon them with satisfaction.

Thus the archfiend clothes with his own attributes the Creator and Benefactor of mankind. Cruelty is satanic. God is love; and all that He created was pure, holy, and lovely, until sin was brought in by the first great rebel. Satan himself is the enemy who tempts man to sin, and then destroys him if he can; and when he has made sure of his victim, then he exults in the ruin he has wrought. If permitted, he would sweep the entire race into his net. Were it not for the interposition of divine power, not one son or daughter of Adam would escape.

Satan is seeking to overcome men today, as he overcame our first parents, by shaking their confidence in their Creator and leading them to doubt the wisdom of His government and the justice of His laws. Satan and his emissaries represent God as even worse than themselves, in order to justify their own malignity and rebellion. The great deceiver endeavors to shift his own horrible cruelty of character upon our heavenly Father, that he may cause himself to appear as one greatly wronged by his expulsion from heaven because he would not submit to so unjust a governor. He presents before the world the liberty which they may enjoy under his mild sway, in contrast with the bondage imposed by the stern decrees of Jehovah. Thus he succeeds in luring souls away from their allegiance to God.

How repugnant to every emotion of love and mercy, and even to our sense of justice, is the doctrine that the wicked dead are tormented with fire and brimstone in an eternally burning hell; that for the sins of a brief earthly life they are to suffer torture as long as God shall live. Yet this doctrine has been widely taught and is still embodied in many of the creeds of Christendom. Said a learned doctor of divinity: "The sight of hell torments will exalt the happiness of the saints forever. When they see others who are of the same nature and born under the same circumstances, plunged in such misery, and they so distinguished, it will make them sensible of how happy they are." Another used these words: "While the decree of reprobation is eternally executing on the vessels of wrath, the smoke of their torment will be eternally ascending in view of the vessels of mercy, who, instead of taking the part of these miserable objects, will say, Amen, Alleluia! praise ye the Lord!"

Where, in the pages of God's word, is such teaching to be found? Will the redeemed in heaven be lost to all emotions of pity and compassion, and even to feelings of common humanity? Are these to be exchanged for the indifference of the stoic or the cruelty of the savage? No, no; such is not the teaching of the Book of God. Those who present the views expressed in the quotations given above may be learned and even honest men, but they are deluded by the sophistry of Satan. He leads them to misconstrue strong expressions of Scripture, giving to the language the coloring of bitterness and malignity which pertains to himself, but not to our Creator. "As I live, saith the Lord God, I have no pleasure in the death of the wicked; but that the wicked turn from his way and live: turn ye, turn ye from your evil ways; for why will ye die?" Ezekiel 33:11.

What would be gained to God should we admit that He delights in witnessing unceasing tortures; that He is regaled with the groans and shrieks and imprecations of the suffering creatures whom He holds in the flames of hell? Can these horrid sounds be music in the ear of Infinite Love? It is urged that the infliction of endless misery upon the wicked would show God's hatred of sin as an evil which is ruinous to the peace and order of the universe. Oh, dreadful blasphemy! As if God's hatred of sin is the reason why it is perpetuated. For, according to the teachings of these theologians, continued torture without hope of mercy maddens its wretched victims, and as they pour out their rage in curses and blasphemy, they are forever augmenting their load of guilt. God's glory is not enhanced by thus perpetuating continually increasing sin through ceaseless ages.

It is beyond the power of the human mind to estimate the evil which has been wrought by the heresy of eternal torment. The religion of the Bible, full of love and goodness, and abounding in compassion, is darkened by superstition and clothed with terror. When we consider in what false colors Satan has painted the character of God, can we wonder that our merciful Creator is feared, dreaded, and even hated? The appalling views of God which have spread over the world from the teachings of the pulpit have made thousands, yes, millions, of skeptics and infidels.

The theory of eternal torment is one of the false doctrines that constitute the wine of the abomination of Babylon, of which she makes all nations drink. Revelation 14:8; 17:2. That ministers of Christ should have accepted this heresy and proclaimed it from the sacred desk is indeed a mystery. They received it from Rome, as they received the false sabbath. True, it has been taught by great and good men; but the light on this subject had not come to them as it has come to us. They were responsible only for the light which shone in their time; we are accountable for that which shines in our day. If we turn from the testimony of God's word, and accept false doctrines because our fathers taught them, we fall under the condemnation pronounced upon Babylon; we are drinking of the wine of her abomination.

A large class to whom the doctrine of eternal torment is revolting are driven to the opposite error. They see that the Scriptures represent God as a being of love and compassion, and they cannot believe that He will consign His creatures to the fires of an eternally burning hell. But holding that the soul is naturally immortal, they see no alternative but to conclude that all mankind will finally be saved. Many regard the threatenings of the Bible as designed merely to frighten men into obedience, and not to be literally fulfilled. Thus the sinner can live in selfish pleasure, disregarding the requirements of God, and yet expect to be finally received into His favor. Such a doctrine, presuming upon God's mercy, but ignoring His justice, pleases the carnal heart and emboldens the wicked in their iniquity.

To show how believers in universal salvation wrest the Scriptures to sustain their soul-destroying dogmas, it is needful only to cite their own utterances. At the funeral of an irreligious young man, who had been killed instantly by an accident, a Universalist minister selected as his text the Scripture statement concerning David: "He was comforted concerning Amnon, seeing he was dead." 2 Samuel 13:39.

"I am frequently asked," said the speaker, "what will be the fate of those who leave the world in sin, die, perhaps, in a state of inebriation, die with the scarlet stains of crime unwashed from their robes, or die as this young man died, having never made a profession or enjoyed an experience of religion. We are content with the Scriptures; their answer shall solve the awful problem. Amnon was exceedingly sinful; he was unrepentant, he was made drunk, and while drunk was killed. David was a prophet of God; he must have known whether it would be ill or well for Amnon in the world to come. What were the expressions of his heart? 'The soul of King David longed to go forth unto Absalom: for he was comforted concerning Amnon, seeing he was dead.' Verse 39.

"And what is the inference to be deduced from this language? Is it not that endless suffering formed no part of his religious belief? So we conceive; and here we discover a triumphant argument in support of the more pleasing, more enlightened, more benevolent hypothesis of ultimate universal purity and peace. He was comforted, seeing his son was dead. And why so? Because by the eye of prophecy he could look forward into the glorious future and see that son far removed from all temptations, released from the bondage and purified from the corruptions of sin, and after being made sufficiently holy and enlightened, admitted to the assembly of ascended and rejoicing spirits. His only comfort was that, in being removed from the present state of sin and suffering, his beloved son had gone where the loftiest breathings of the Holy Spirit would be shed upon his darkened soul, where his mind would be unfolded to the wisdom of heaven and the sweet raptures of immortal love, and thus prepared with a sanctified nature to enjoy the rest and society of the heavenly inheritance.

"In these thoughts we would be understood to believe that the salvation of heaven depends upon nothing which we can do in this life; neither upon a present change of heart, nor upon present belief, or a present profession of religion."

Thus does the professed minister of Christ reiterate the falsehood uttered by the serpent in Eden: "Ye shall not surely die." "In the day ye eat thereof, then your eyes shall be opened, and ye shall be as gods." He declares that the vilest of sinners—the murderer, the thief, and the adulterer—will after death be prepared to enter into immortal bliss.

And from what does this perverter of the Scriptures draw his conclusions? From a single sentence expressing David's submission to the dispensation of Providence. His soul "longed to go forth unto Absalom; for he was comforted concerning Amnon, seeing he was dead." The poignancy of his grief having been softened by time, his thoughts turned from the dead to the living son, self-banished through fear of the just punishment of his crime. And this is the evidence that the incestuous, drunken Amnon was at death immediately transported to the abodes of bliss, there to be purified and prepared for the companionship of sinless angels! A pleasing fable indeed, well suited to gratify the carnal heart! This is Satan's own doctrine, and it does his work effectually. Should we be surprised that, with such instruction, wickedness abounds?

The course pursued by this one false teacher illustrates that of many others. A few words of Scripture are separated from the context, which would in many cases show their meaning to be exactly opposite to the interpretation put upon them; and such disjointed passages are perverted and used in proof of doctrines that have no foundation in the word of God. The testimony cited as evidence that the drunken Amnon is in heaven is a mere inference directly contradicted by the plain and positive statement of the Scriptures that no drunkard shall inherit the kingdom of God. 1 Corinthians 6:10. It is thus that doubters, unbelievers, and skeptics turn the truth into a lie. And multitudes have been deceived by their sophistry and rocked to sleep in the cradle of carnal security.

If it were true that the souls of all men passed directly to heaven at the hour of dissolution, then we might well covet death rather than life. Many have been led by this belief to put an end to their existence.

When overwhelmed with trouble, perplexity, and disappointment, it seems an easy thing to break the brittle thread of life and soar away into the bliss of the eternal world.

God has given in His word decisive evidence that He will punish the transgressors of His law. Those who flatter themselves that He is too merciful to execute justice upon the sinner, have only to look to the cross of Calvary. The death of the spotless Son of God testifies that "the wages of sin is death," that every violation of God's law must receive its just retribution. Christ the sinless became sin for man. He bore the guilt of transgression, and the hiding of His Father's face, until His heart was broken and His life crushed out. All this sacrifice was made that sinners might be redeemed. In no other way could man be freed from the penalty of sin. And every soul that refuses to become a partaker of the atonement provided at such a cost must bear in his own person the guilt and punishment of transgression.

Let us consider what the Bible teaches further concerning the ungodly and unrepentant, whom the Universalist places in heaven as holy, happy angels.

"I will give unto him that is athirst of the fountain of the water of life freely." Revelation 21:6. This promise is only to those that thirst. None but those who feel their need of the water of life, and seek it at the loss of all things else, will be supplied. "He that overcometh shall inherit all things; and I will be his God, and he shall be My son." Verse 7. Here, also, conditions are specified. In order to inherit all things, we must resist and overcome sin.

The Lord declares by the prophet Isaiah: "Say ye to the righteous, that it shall be well with him." "Woe unto the wicked! it shall be ill with him: for the reward of his hands shall be given him." Isaiah 3:10, 11. "Though a sinner do evil an hundred times," says the wise man, "and his days be prolonged, yet surely I know that it shall be well with them that fear God, which fear before Him: but it shall not be well with the wicked." Ecclesiastes 8:12, 13. And Paul testifies that the sinner is treasuring up unto himself "wrath against the day of wrath and revelation of the righteous judgment of God; who will render to every man according to his deeds;" "tribulation and anguish upon every soul of man that doeth evil." Romans 2:5,6,9.

"No fornicator, nor unclean person, nor covetous man, who is an idolater, hath any inheritance in the kingdom of Christ and God."

Ephesians 5:5, A.R.V. "Follow peace with all men, and holiness, without which no man shall see the Lord." Hebrews 12:14. "Blessed are they that do His commandments, that they may have right to the tree of life, and may enter in through the gates into the city. For without are dogs, and sorcerers, and whoremongers, and murderers, and idolaters, and whosoever loveth and maketh a lie." Revelation 22:14, 15.

God has given to men a declaration of His character and of His method of dealing with sin. "The Lord God, merciful and gracious, long-suffering and abundant in goodness and truth, keeping mercy for thousands, forgiving iniquity and transgression and sin, and that will by no means clear the guilty." Exodus 34:6, 7. "All the wicked will He destroy." "The transgressors shall be destroyed together: the end of the wicked shall be cut off." Psalms 145:20; 37:38. The power and authority of the divine government will be employed to put down rebellion; yet all the manifestations of retributive justice will be perfectly consistent with the character of God as a merciful, long-suffering, benevolent being.

God does not force the will or judgment of any. He takes no pleasure in a slavish obedience. He desires that the creatures of His hands shall love Him because He is worthy of love. He would have them obey Him because they have an intelligent appreciation of His wisdom, justice, and benevolence. And all who have a just conception of these qualities will love Him because they are drawn toward Him in admiration of His attributes.

The principles of kindness, mercy, and love, taught and exemplified by our Saviour, are a transcript of the will and character of God. Christ declared that He taught nothing except that which He had received from His Father. The principles of the divine government are in perfect harmony with the Saviour's precept, "Love your enemies." God executes justice upon the wicked, for the good of the universe, and even for the good of those upon whom His judgments are visited. He would make them happy if He could do so in accordance with the laws of His government and the justice of His character. He surrounds them with the tokens of His love, He grants them a knowledge of His law, and follows them with the offers of His mercy; but they despise His love, make void His law, and reject His mercy. While constantly receiving His gifts, they dishonor the Giver; they hate God because they know that He abhors their sins. The Lord bears long with their perversity; but the decisive hour will come at last, when their destiny is to be decided. Will He then chain these rebels to His side? Will He force them to do His will?

Those who have chosen Satan as their leader and have been controlled by his power are not prepared to enter the presence of God. Pride, deception, licentiousness, cruelty, have become fixed in their characters. Can they enter heaven to dwell forever with those whom they despised and hated on earth? Truth will never be agreeable to a liar; meekness will not satisfy self-esteem and pride; purity is not acceptable to the corrupt; disinterested love does not appear attractive to the selfish. What source of enjoyment could heaven offer to those who are wholly absorbed in earthly and selfish interests?

Could those whose lives have been spent in rebellion against God be suddenly transported to heaven and witness the high, the holy state of perfection that ever exists there,—every soul filled with love, every countenance beaming with joy, enrapturing music in melodious strains rising in honor of God and the Lamb, and ceaseless streams of light flowing upon the redeemed from the face of Him who sitteth upon the throne,—could those whose hearts are filled with hatred of God, of truth and holiness, mingle with the heavenly throng and join their songs of praise? Could they endure the glory of God and the Lamb? No, no; years of probation were granted them, that they might form characters for heaven; but they have never trained the mind to love purity; they have never learned the language of heaven, and now it is too late. A life of rebellion against God has unfitted them for heaven. Its purity, holiness, and peace would be torture to them; the glory of God would be a consuming fire. They would long to flee from that holy place. They would welcome destruction, that they might be hidden from the face of Him who died to redeem them. The destiny of the wicked is fixed by their own choice. Their exclusion from heaven is voluntary with themselves, and just and merciful on the part of God.

Like the waters of the Flood the fires of the great day declare God's verdict that the wicked are incurable. They have no disposition to submit to divine authority. Their will has been exercised in revolt; and when life is ended, it is too late to turn the current of their thoughts in the opposite direction, too late to turn from transgression to obedience, from hatred to love.

In sparing the life of Cain the murderer, God gave the world an example of what would be the result of permitting the sinner to live to continue a course of unbridled iniquity. Through the influence of Cain's teaching and example, multitudes of his descendants were led into sin, until "the wickedness of man was great in the earth" and "every imagination of the thoughts of his heart was only evil continually." "The earth also was corrupt before God, and the earth was filled with violence." Genesis 6:5, 11.

In mercy to the world, God blotted out its wicked inhabitants in Noah's time. In mercy He destroyed the corrupt dwellers in Sodom. Through the deceptive power of Satan the workers of iniquity obtain sympathy and admiration, and are thus constantly leading others to rebellion. It was so in Cain's and in Noah's day, and in the time of Abraham and Lot; it is so in our time. It is in mercy to the universe that God will finally destroy the rejecters of His grace.

"The wages of sin is death; but the gift of God is eternal life through Jesus Christ our Lord." Romans 6:23. While life is the inheritance of the righteous, death is the portion of the wicked. Moses declared to Israel: "I have set before thee this day life and good, and death and evil." Deuteronomy 30:15. The death referred to in these scriptures is not that pronounced upon Adam, for all mankind suffer the penalty of his transgression. It is "the second death" that is placed in contrast with everlasting life.

In consequence of Adam's sin, death passed upon the whole human race. All alike go down into the grave. And through the provisions of the plan of salvation, all are to be brought forth from their graves. "There shall be a resurrection of the dead, both of the just and unjust;" "for as in Adam all die, even so in Christ shall all be made alive." Acts 24:15; 1 Corinthians 15:22. But a distinction is made between the two classes that are brought forth. "All that are in the graves shall hear His voice, and shall come forth; they that have done good, unto the resurrection of life; and they that have done evil, unto the resurrection of damnation." John 5:28, 29. They who have been "accounted worthy" of the resurrection of life are "blessed and holy." "On such the second death hath no power." Revelation 20:6. But those who have not, through repentance and faith, secured pardon, must receive the penalty of transgression—"the wages of sin." They suffer punishment varying in duration and intensity, "according to their works," but finally ending in the second death. Since it is impossible for God, consistently with His justice and mercy, to save the sinner in his sins, He deprives him of the existence which his transgressions have forfeited and of which he has proved himself unworthy. Says an inspired writer: "Yet a little while, and the wicked shall not be: yea, thou shalt diligently consider his place, and it shall not be." And another declares: "They shall be as though they had not been." Psalm 37:10; Obadiah 16. Covered with infamy, they sink into hopeless, eternal oblivion.

Thus will be made an end of sin, with all the woe and ruin which have resulted from it. Says the psalmist: "Thou hast destroyed the wicked, Thou hast put out their name forever and ever. O thou enemy, destructions are come to a perpetual end." Psalm 9:5, 6. John, in the Revelation, looking forward to the eternal state, hears a universal anthem of praise undisturbed by one note of discord. Every creature in heaven and earth was heard ascribing glory to God. Revelation 5:13. There will then be no lost souls to blaspheme God as they writhe in never-ending torment; no wretched beings in hell will mingle their shrieks with the songs of the saved.

Upon the fundamental error of natural immortality rests the doctrine of consciousness in death—a doctrine, like eternal torment, opposed to the teachings of the Scriptures, to the dictates of reason, and to our feelings of humanity. According to the popular belief, the redeemed in heaven are acquainted with all that takes place on the earth and especially with the lives of the friends whom they have left behind. But how could it be a source of happiness to the dead to know the troubles of the living, to witness the sins committed by their own loved ones, and to see them enduring all the sorrows, disappointments, and anguish of life? How much of heaven's bliss would be enjoyed by those who were hovering over their friends on earth? And how utterly revolting is the belief that as soon as the breath leaves the body the soul of the impenitent is consigned to the flames of hell! To what depths of anguish must those be plunged who see their friends passing to the grave unprepared, to enter upon an eternity of woe and sin! Many have been driven to insanity by this harrowing thought.

What say the Scriptures concerning these things? David declares that man is not conscious in death. "His breath goeth forth, he returneth to his earth; in that very day his thoughts perish." Psalm 146:4. Solomon bears the same testimony: "The living know that they shall die: but the dead know not anything." "Their love, and their hatred, and their envy, is now perished; neither have they any more a portion forever in anything that is done under the sun." "There is no work, nor device, nor knowledge, nor wisdom, in the grave, whither thou goest." Ecclesiastes 9:5, 6, 10.

When, in answer to his prayer, Hezekiah's life was prolonged fifteen years, the grateful king rendered to God a tribute of praise for His great mercy. In this song he tells the reason why he thus rejoices: "The grave cannot praise Thee, death cannot celebrate Thee: they that go down into the pit cannot hope for Thy truth. The living, the living, he shall praise Thee, as I do this day." Isaiah 38:18, 19. Popular theology represents the righteous dead as in heaven, entered into bliss and praising God with an immortal tongue; but Hezekiah could see no such glorious prospect in death. With his words agrees the testimony of the psalmist: "In death there is no remembrance of Thee: in the grave who shall give Thee thanks?" "The dead praise not the Lord, neither any that go down into silence." Psalms 6:5; 115:17.

Peter on the Day of Pentecost declared that the patriarch David "is both dead and buried, and his sepulcher is with us unto this day." "For David is not ascended into the heavens." Acts 2:29, 34. The fact that David remains in the grave until the resurrection proves that the righteous do not go to heaven at death. It is only through the resurrection, and by virtue of the fact that Christ has risen, that David can at last sit at the right hand of God.

And said Paul: "If the dead rise not, then is not Christ raised: and if Christ be not raised, your faith is vain; ye are yet in your sins. Then they also which are fallen asleep in Christ are perished." 1 Corinthians 15:16-18. If for four thousand years the righteous had gone directly to heaven at death, how could Paul have said that if there is no resurrection, "they also which are fallen asleep in Christ are perished"? No resurrection would be necessary.

The martyr Tyndale, referring to the state of the dead, declared: "I confess openly, that I am not persuaded that they be already in the full glory that Christ is in, or the elect angels of God are in. Neither is it any article of my faith; for if it were so, I see not but then the preaching of the resurrection of the flesh were a thing in vain."—William Tyndale, Preface to New Testament (ed. 1534). Reprinted in *British Reformers—Tindal, Frith, Barnes*, page 349.

It is an undeniable fact that the hope of immortal blessedness at death has led to a widespread neglect of the Bible doctrine of the resurrection. This tendency was remarked by Dr. Adam Clarke, who said: "The doctrine of the resurrection appears to have been thought of much more consequence among the primitive Christians than it is *now*! How is this? The apostles were continually insisting on it, and exciting the followers of God to diligence, obedience, and cheerfulness through it. And their successors in the present day seldom mention it! So apostles preached, and so primitive Christians believed; so we preach, and so our hearers believe. There is not a doctrine in the gospel on which more stress is laid; and there is not a doctrine in the present system of preaching which is treated with more neglect!"—*Commentary*, remarks on 1 Corinthians 15, paragraph 3.

This has continued until the glorious truth of the resurrection has been almost wholly obscured and lost sight of by the Christian world. Thus a leading religious writer, commenting on the words of Paul in 1 Thessalonians 4:13-18, says: "For all practical purposes of comfort the doctrine of the blessed immortality of the righteous takes the place for us of any doubtful doctrine of the Lord's second coming. At our death the Lord comes for us. That is what we are to wait and watch for. The dead are already passed into glory. They do not wait for the trump for their judgment and blessedness."

But when about to leave His disciples, Jesus did not tell them that they would soon come to Him. "I go to prepare a place for you," He said. "And if I go and prepare a place for you, I will come again, and receive you unto Myself." John 14:2, 3. And Paul tells us, further, that "the Lord Himself shall descend from heaven with a shout, with the voice of the Archangel, and with the trump of God: and the dead in Christ shall rise first: then we which are alive and remain shall be caught up together with them in the clouds, to meet the Lord in the air: and so shall we ever be with the Lord." And he adds: "Comfort one another with these words." 1 Thessalonians 4:16-18. How wide the contrast between these words of comfort and those of the Universalist minister previously quoted! The latter consoled the bereaved friends with the assurance that, however sinful the dead might have been, when he breathed out his life here he was to be received among the angels. Paul points his brethren to the future coming of the Lord, when the fetters of the tomb shall be broken, and the "dead in Christ" shall be raised to eternal life.

Before any can enter the mansions of the blessed, their cases must be investigated, and their characters and their deeds must pass in review before God. All are to be judged according to the things written in the books and to be rewarded as their works have been. This judgment does not take place at death. Mark the words of Paul: "He hath appointed a day, in the which He will judge the world in righteousness by that Man whom He hath ordained; whereof He hath given assurance unto all men, in that He hath raised Him from the dead." Acts 17:31. Here the apostle plainly stated that a specified time, then future, had been fixed upon for the judgment of the world.

Jude refers to the same period: "The angels which kept not their first estate, but left their own habitation, He hath reserved in everlasting chains under darkness unto the judgment of the great day." And, again, he quotes the words of Enoch: "Behold, the Lord cometh with ten thousands of His saints, to execute judgment upon all." Jude 6, 14, 15. John declares that he "saw the dead, small and great, stand before God; and the books were opened: ... and the dead were judged out of those things which were written in the books." Revelation 20:12.

But if the dead are already enjoying the bliss of heaven or writhing in the flames of hell, what need of a future judgment? The teachings of God's word on these important points are neither obscure nor contradictory; they may be understood by common minds. But what candid mind can see either wisdom or justice in the current theory? Will the righteous, after the investigation of their cases at the judgment, receive the commendation, "Well done, thou good and faithful servant: ... *enter thou* into the joy of thy Lord," when they have been dwelling in His presence, perhaps for long ages? Are the wicked summoned from the place of torment to receive sentence from the Judge of all the earth: "Depart from Me, ye cursed, into everlasting fire"? Matthew 25:21, 41. Oh, solemn mockery! shameful impeachment of the wisdom and justice of God!

The theory of the immortality of the soul was one of those false doctrines that Rome, borrowing from paganism, incorporated into the religion of Christendom. Martin Luther classed it with the "monstrous fables that form part of the Roman dunghill of decretals."—E. Petavel, *The Problem of Immortality*, page 255. Commenting on the words of Solomon in Ecclesiastes, that the dead know not anything, the Reformer says: "Another place proving that the dead have no ... feeling. There is, saith he, no duty, no science, no knowledge, no wisdom there. Solomon judgeth that the dead are asleep, and feel nothing at all. For the dead lie there, accounting neither days nor years, but when they are awaked, they shall seem to have slept scarce one minute."—Martin Luther, *Exposition of Solomon's Booke Called Ecclesiastes*, page 152.

Nowhere in the Sacred Scriptures is found the statement that the righteous go to their reward or the wicked to their punishment at death. The patriarchs and prophets have left no such assurance. Christ and His apostles have given no hint of it. The Bible clearly teaches that the dead do not go immediately to heaven. They are represented as sleeping until the resurrection. 1 Thessalonians 4:14; Job 14:10-12. In the very day when the silver cord is loosed and the golden bowl broken (Ecclesiastes 12:6), man's thoughts perish. They that go down to the grave are in silence. They know no more of anything that is done under the sun. Job 14:21. Blessed rest for the weary righteous! Time, be it long or short, is but a moment to them. They sleep; they are awakened by the trump of God to a glorious immortality. "For the trumpet shall sound, and the dead shall be raised incorruptible. ... So when this corruptible shall have put on incorruption, and this mortal shall have put on immortality, then shall be brought to pass the saying that is written, Death is swallowed up in victory." 1 Corinthians 15:52-54. As they are called forth from their deep slumber they begin to think just where they ceased. The last sensation was the pang of death; the last thought, that they were falling beneath the power of the grave. When they arise from the tomb, their first glad thought will be echoed in the triumphal shout: "O death, where is thy sting? O grave, where is thy victory?" Verse 55.

Eight

—Can Our Dead Speak to Us?—

T he ministration of holy angels, as presented in the Scriptures, is a truth most comforting and precious to every follower of Christ. But the Bible teaching upon this point has been obscured and perverted by the errors of popular theology. The doctrine of natural immortality, first borrowed from the pagan philosophy, and in the darkness of the great apostasy incorporated into the Christian faith, has supplanted the truth, so plainly taught in Scripture, that "the dead know not anything." Multitudes have come to believe that it is spirits of the dead who are the "ministering spirits, sent forth to minister for them who shall be heirs of salvation." And this notwithstanding the testimony of Scripture to the existence of heavenly angels, and their connection with the history of man, before the death of a human being.

The doctrine of man's consciousness in death, especially the belief that spirits of the dead return to minister to the living, has prepared the way for modern spiritualism. If the dead are admitted to the presence of God and holy angels, and privileged with knowledge far exceeding what they before possessed, why should they not return to the earth to enlighten and instruct the living? If, as taught by popular theologians, spirits of the dead are hovering about their friends on earth, why should they not be permitted to communicate with them, to warn them against evil, or to comfort them in sorrow? How can those who believe in man's consciousness in death reject what comes to them as divine light communicated by glorified spirits? Here is a channel regarded as sacred, through which Satan works for the accomplishment of his purposes. The fallen angels who do his bidding appear as messengers from the spirit world. While professing to bring the living into communication with the dead, the prince of evil exercises his bewitching influence upon their minds.

He has power to bring before men the appearance of their departed friends. The counterfeit is perfect; the familiar look, the words, the tone, are reproduced with marvelous distinctness. Many are comforted with the assurance that their loved ones are enjoying the bliss of heaven, and without suspicion of danger, they give ear "to seducing spirits, and doctrines of devils."

When they have been led to believe that the dead actually return to communicate with them, Satan causes those to appear who went into the grave unprepared. They claim to be happy in heaven and even to occupy exalted positions there, and thus the error is widely taught that no difference is made between the righteous and the wicked. The pretended visitants from the world of spirits sometimes utter cautions and warnings which prove to be correct. Then, as confidence is gained, they present doctrines that directly undermine faith in the Scriptures. With an appearance of deep interest in the well-being of their friends on earth, they insinuate the most dangerous errors. The fact that they state some truths, and are able at times to foretell future events, gives to their statements an appearance of reliability; and their false teachings are accepted by the multitudes as readily, and believed as implicitly, as if they were the most sacred truths of the Bible. The law of God is set aside, the Spirit of grace despised, the blood of the covenant counted an unholy thing. The spirits deny the deity of Christ and place even the Creator on a level with themselves. Thus under a new disguise the great rebel still carries on his warfare against God, begun in heaven and for nearly six thousand years continued upon the earth.

Many endeavor to account for spiritual manifestations by attributing them wholly to fraud and sleight of hand on the part of the medium. But while it is true that the results of trickery have often been palmed off as genuine manifestations, there have been, also, marked exhibitions of supernatural power. The mysterious rapping with which modern spiritualism began was not the result of human trickery or cunning, but was the direct work of evil angels, who thus introduced one of the most successful of soul-destroying delusions. Many will be ensnared through the belief that spiritualism is a merely human imposture; when brought face to face with manifestations which they cannot but regard as supernatural, they will be deceived, and will be led to accept them as the great power of God.

These persons overlook the testimony of the Scriptures concerning the wonders wrought by Satan and his agents. It was by satanic aid that Pharaoh's magicians were enabled to counterfeit the work of God. Paul testifies that before the second advent of Christ there will be similar manifestations of satanic power. The coming of the Lord is to be preceded by "the working of Satan with all power and signs and lying wonders, and with all deceivableness of unrighteousness." 2 Thessalonians 2:9, 10. And the apostle John, describing the miracle-working power that will be manifested in the last days, declares: "He doeth great wonders, so that he maketh fire come down from heaven on the earth in the sight of men, and deceiveth them that dwell on the earth by the means of those miracles which he had power to do." Revelation 13:13, 14. No mere impostures are here foretold. Men are deceived by the miracles which Satan's agents have power to do, not which they pretend to do.

The prince of darkness, who has so long bent the powers of his mastermind to the work of deception, skillfully adapts his temptations to men of all classes and conditions. To persons of culture and refinement he presents spiritualism in its more refined and intellectual aspects, and thus succeeds in drawing many into his snare. The wisdom which spiritualism imparts is that described by the apostle James, which "descendeth not from above, but is earthly, sensual, devilish." James 3:15. This, however, the great deceiver conceals when concealment will best suit his purpose. He who could appear clothed with the brightness of the heavenly seraphs before Christ in the wilderness of temptation, comes to men in the most attractive manner as an angel of light. He appeals to the reason by the presentation of elevating themes; he delights the fancy with enrapturing scenes; and he enlists the affections by his eloquent portrayals of love and charity. He excites the imagination to lofty flights, leading men to take so great pride in their own wisdom that in their hearts they despise the Eternal One. That mighty being who could take the world's Redeemer to an exceedingly high mountain and bring before Him all the kingdoms of the earth and the glory of them, will present his temptations to men in a manner to pervert the senses of all who are not shielded by divine power.

Satan beguiles men now as he beguiled Eve in Eden by flattery, by kindling a desire to obtain forbidden knowledge, by exciting ambition for self-exaltation. It was cherishing these evils that caused his fall, and through them he aims to compass the ruin of men. "Ye shall be as gods," he declares, "knowing good and evil." Genesis 3:5. Spiritualism teaches "that man is the creature of progression; that it is his destiny from his birth to progress, even to eternity, toward the Godhead." And again: "Each mind will judge itself and not another." "The judgment will be right, because it is the judgment of self. ... The throne is within you." Said a spiritualistic teacher, as the "spiritual consciousness" awoke within him: "My fellow men, all were unfallen demigods." And another declares: "Any just and perfect being is Christ."

Thus, in place of the righteousness and perfection of the infinite God, the true object of adoration; in place of the perfect righteousness of His law, the true standard of human attainment, Satan has substituted the sinful, erring nature of man himself as the only object of adoration, the only rule of judgment, or standard of character. This is progress, not upward, but downward.

It is a law both of the intellectual and the spiritual nature that by beholding we become changed. The mind gradually adapts itself to the subjects upon which it is allowed to dwell. It becomes assimilated to that which it is accustomed to love and reverence. Man will never rise higher than his standard of purity or goodness or truth. If self is his loftiest ideal, he will never attain to anything more exalted. Rather, he will constantly sink lower and lower. The grace of God alone has power to exalt man. Left to himself, his course must inevitably be downward.

To the self-indulgent, the pleasure-loving, the sensual, spiritualism presents itself under a less subtle disguise than to the more refined and intellectual; in its grosser forms they find that which is in harmony with their inclinations. Satan studies every indication of the frailty of human nature, he marks the sins which each individual is inclined to commit, and then he takes care that opportunities shall not be wanting to gratify the tendency to evil. He tempts men to excess in that which is in itself lawful, causing them, through intemperance, to weaken physical, mental, and moral power. He has destroyed and is destroying thousands through the indulgence of the passions, thus brutalizing the entire nature of man. And to complete his work, he declares, through the spirits that "true knowledge places man above all law;" that "whatever is, is right;" that "God doth not condemn;" and that "*all* sins which are committed are innocent." When the people are thus led to believe that desire is the highest law, that liberty is license, and that man is accountable only to himself, who can wonder that corruption and depravity teem on every hand? Multitudes eagerly accept teachings that leave them at liberty to obey the promptings of the carnal heart. The reins of self-control are laid upon the neck of lust, the powers of mind and soul are made subject to the animal propensities, and Satan exultingly sweeps into his net thousands who profess to be followers of Christ.

But none need be deceived by the lying claims of spiritualism. God has given the world sufficient light to enable them to discover the snare. As already shown, the theory which forms the very foundation of spiritualism is at war with the plainest statements of Scripture. The Bible declares that the dead know not anything, that their thoughts have perished; they have no part in anything that is done under the sun; they know nothing of the joys or sorrows of those who were dearest to them on earth.

Furthermore, God has expressly forbidden all pretended communication with departed spirits. In the days of the Hebrews there was a class of people who claimed, as do the spiritualists of today, to hold communication with the dead. But the "familiar spirits," as these visitants from other worlds were called, are declared by the Bible to be "the spirits of devils." (Compare Numbers 25:1-3; Psalm 106:28; 1 Corinthians 10:20; Revelation 16:14.) The work of dealing with familiar spirits was pronounced an abomination to the Lord, and was solemnly forbidden under penalty of death. Leviticus 19:31; 20:27. The very name of witchcraft is now held in contempt. The claim that men can hold intercourse with evil spirits is regarded as a fable of the Dark Ages. But spiritualism, which numbers its converts by hundreds of thousands, yea, by millions, which has made its way into scientific circles, which has invaded churches, and has found favor in legislative bodies, and even in the courts of kings—this mammoth deception is but a revival, in a new disguise, of the witchcraft condemned and prohibited of old.

If there were no other evidence of the real character of spiritualism, it should be enough for the Christian that the spirits make no difference between righteousness and sin, between the noblest and purest of the apostles of Christ and the most corrupt of the servants of Satan. By representing the basest of men as in heaven, and highly exalted there, Satan says to the world: "No matter how wicked you are; no matter whether you believe or disbelieve God and the Bible. Live as you please; heaven is your home." The spiritualist teachers virtually declare: "Everyone that doeth evil is good in the sight of the Lord, and He delighteth in them; or, Where is the God of judgment?" Malachi 2:17. Saith the word of God: "Woe unto them that call evil good, and good evil; that put darkness for light, and light for darkness." Isaiah 5:20.

The apostles, as personated by these lying spirits, are made to contradict what they wrote at the dictation of the Holy Spirit when on earth. They deny the divine origin of the Bible, and thus tear away the foundation of the Christian's hope and put out the light that reveals the way to heaven. Satan is making the world believe that the Bible is a mere fiction, or at least a book suited to the infancy of the race, but now to be lightly regarded, or cast aside as obsolete. And to take the place of the word of God he holds out spiritual manifestations. Here is a channel wholly under his control; by this means he can make the world believe what he will. The Book that is to judge him and his followers he puts in the shade, just where he wants it; the Saviour of the world he makes to be no more than a common man. And as the Roman guard that watched the tomb of Jesus spread the lying report which the priests and elders put into their mouths to disprove His resurrection, so do the believers in spiritual manifestations try to make it appear that there is nothing miraculous in the circumstances of our Saviour's life. After thus seeking to put Jesus in the background, they call attention to their own miracles, declaring that these far exceed the works of Christ.

It is true that spiritualism is now changing its form and, veiling some of its more objectionable features, is assuming a Christian guise. But its utterances from the platform and the press have been before the public for many years, and in these its real character stands revealed. These teachings cannot be denied or hidden.

Even in its present form, so far from being more worthy of toleration than formerly, it is really a more dangerous, because a more subtle, deception. While it formerly denounced Christ and the Bible, it now *professes* to accept both. But the Bible is interpreted in a manner that is pleasing to the unrenewed heart, while its solemn and vital truths are made of no effect. Love is dwelt upon as the chief attribute of God, but it is degraded to a weak sentimentalism, making little distinction between good and evil. God's justice, His denunciations of sin, the requirements of His holy law, are all kept out of sight. The people are taught to regard the Decalogue as a dead letter. Pleasing, bewitching fables captivate the senses and lead men to reject the Bible as the foundation of their faith. Christ is as verily denied as before; but Satan has so blinded the eyes of the people that the deception is not discerned.

There are few who have any just conception of the deceptive power of spiritualism and the danger of coming under its influence. Many tamper with it merely to gratify their curiosity. They have no real faith in it and would be filled with horror at the thought of yielding themselves to the spirits' control. But they venture upon the forbidden ground, and the mighty destroyer exercises his power upon them against their will. Let them once be induced to submit their minds to his direction, and he holds them captive. It is impossible, in their own strength, to break away from the bewitching, alluring spell. Nothing but the power of God, granted in answer to the earnest prayer of faith, can deliver these ensnared souls.

All who indulge sinful traits of character, or willfully cherish a known sin, are inviting the temptations of Satan. They separate themselves from God and from the watchcare of His angels; as the evil one presents his deceptions, they are without defense and fall an easy prey. Those who thus place themselves in his power little realize where their course will end. Having achieved their overthrow, the tempter will employ them as his agents to lure others to ruin.

Says the prophet Isaiah: "When they shall say unto you, Seek unto them that have familiar spirits, and unto wizards that peep, and that mutter: should not a people seek unto their God? for the living to the dead? To the law and to the testimony: if they speak not according to this word, it is because there is no light in them." Isaiah 8:19, 20. If men had been willing to receive the truth so plainly stated in the Scriptures concerning the nature of man and the state of the dead, they would see in the claims and manifestations of spiritualism the working of Satan with power and signs and lying wonders. But rather than yield the liberty so agreeable to the carnal heart, and renounce the sins which they love, multitudes close their eyes to the light and walk straight on, regardless of warnings, while Satan weaves his snares about them, and they become his prey. "Because they received not the love of the truth, that they might be saved," therefore "God shall send them strong delusion, that they should believe a lie." 2 Thessalonians 2:10, 11.

Those who oppose the teachings of spiritualism are assailing, not men alone, but Satan and his angels. They have entered upon a contest against principalities and powers and wicked spirits in high places. Satan will not yield one inch of ground except as he is driven back by the power of heavenly messengers. The people of God should be able to meet him, as did our Saviour, with the words: "It is written." Satan can quote Scripture now as in the days of Christ, and he will pervert its teachings to sustain his delusions. Those who would stand in this time of peril must understand for themselves the testimony of the Scriptures.

Many will be confronted by the spirits of devils personating beloved relatives or friends and declaring the most dangerous heresies. These visitants will appeal to our tenderest sympathies and will work miracles to sustain their pretensions. We must be prepared to withstand them with the Bible truth that the dead know not anything and that they who thus appear are the spirits of devils.

Just before us is "the hour of temptation, which shall come upon all the world, to try them that dwell upon the earth." Revelation 3:10. All whose faith is not firmly established upon the word of God will be deceived and overcome. Satan "works with all deceivableness of unrighteousness" to gain control of the children of men, and his deceptions will continually increase. But he can gain his object only as men voluntarily yield to his temptations. Those who are earnestly seeking a knowledge of the truth and are striving to purify their souls through obedience, thus doing what they can to prepare for the conflict, will find, in the God of truth, a sure defense. "Because thou hast kept the word of My patience, I also will keep thee" (verse 10), is the Saviour's promise. He would sooner send every angel out of heaven to protect His people than leave one soul that trusts in Him to be overcome by Satan.

The prophet Isaiah brings to view the fearful deception which will come upon the wicked, causing them to count themselves secure from the judgments of God: "We have made a covenant with death, and with hell are we at agreement; when the overflowing scourge shall pass through, it shall not come unto us: for we have made lies our refuge, and under falsehood have we hid ourselves." Isaiah 28:15. In the class here described are included those who in their stubborn impenitence comfort themselves with the assurance that there is to be no punishment for the sinner; that all mankind, it matters not how corrupt, are to be exalted to heaven, to become as the angels of God. But still more emphatically are those making a covenant with death and an agreement with hell, who renounce the truths which Heaven has provided as a defense for the righteous in the day of trouble, and accept the refuge of lies offered by Satan in its stead—the delusive pretensions of spiritualism.

Marvelous beyond expression is the blindness of the people of this generation. Thousands reject the word of God as unworthy of belief and with eager confidence receive the deceptions of Satan. Skeptics and scoffers denounce the bigotry of those who contend for the faith of prophets and apostles, and they divert themselves by holding up to ridicule the solemn declarations of the Scriptures concerning Christ and the plan of salvation, and the retribution to be visited upon the rejecters of the truth. They affect great pity for minds so narrow, weak, and superstitious as to acknowledge the claims of God and obey the requirements of His law. They manifest as much assurance as if, indeed, they had made a covenant with death and an agreement with hell—as if they had erected an impassable, impenetrable barrier between themselves and the vengeance of God. Nothing can arouse their fears. So fully have they yielded to the tempter, so closely are they united with him, and so thoroughly imbued with his spirit, that they have no power and no inclination to break away from his snare.

Satan has long been preparing for his final effort to deceive the world. The foundation of his work was laid by the assurance given to Eve in Eden: "Ye shall not surely die." "In the day ye eat thereof, then your eyes shall be opened, and ye shall be as gods, knowing good and evil." Genesis 3:4, 5. Little by little he has prepared the way for his masterpiece of deception in the development of spiritualism. He has not yet reached the full accomplishment of his designs; but it will be reached in the last remnant of time. Says the prophet: "I saw three unclean spirits like frogs; … they are the spirits of devils, working miracles, which go forth unto the kings of the earth and of the whole world, to gather them to the battle of that great day of God Almighty." Revelation 16:13, 14. Except those who are kept by the power of God, through faith in His word, the whole world will be swept into the ranks of this delusion. The people are fast being lulled to a fatal security, to be awakened only by the outpouring of the wrath of God.

Saith the Lord God: "Judgment also will I lay to the line, and righteousness to the plummet: and the hail shall sweep away the refuge of lies, and the waters shall overflow the hiding place. And your covenant with death shall be disannulled, and your agreement with hell shall not stand; when the overflowing scourge shall pass through, then ye shall be trodden down by it." Isaiah 28:17, 18.

Nine

—Liberty of Conscience Threatened—

Romanism is now regarded by Protestants with far greater favor than in former years. In those countries where Catholicism is not in the ascendancy, and the papists are taking a conciliatory course in order to gain influence, there is an increasing indifference concerning the doctrines that separate the reformed churches from the papal hierarchy; the opinion is gaining ground that, after all, we do not differ so widely upon vital points as has been supposed, and that a little concession on our part will bring us into a better understanding with Rome. The time was when Protestants placed a high value upon the liberty of conscience which had been so dearly purchased. They taught their children to abhor popery and held that to seek harmony with Rome would be disloyalty to God. But how widely different are the sentiments now expressed!

The defenders of the papacy declare that the church has been maligned, and the Protestant world are inclined to accept the statement. Many urge that it is unjust to judge the church of today by the abominations and absurdities that marked her reign during the centuries of ignorance and darkness. They excuse her horrible cruelty as the result of the barbarism of the times and plead that the influence of modern civilization has changed her sentiments.

Have these persons forgotten the claim of infallibility put forth for eight hundred years by this haughty power? So far from being relinquished, this claim was affirmed in the nineteenth century with greater positiveness than ever before. As Rome asserts that the "church *never erred*; nor will it, according to the Scriptures, *ever err*" (John L. von Mosheim, *Institutes of Ecclesiastical History*, book 3, century II, part 2, chapter 2, section 9, note 17), how can she renounce the principles which governed her course in past ages?

The papal church will never relinquish her claim to infallibility. All that she has done in her persecution of those who reject her dogmas she holds to be right; and would she not repeat the same acts, should the opportunity be presented? Let the restraints now imposed by secular governments be removed and Rome be reinstated in her former power, and there would speedily be a revival of her tyranny and persecution.

A well-known writer speaks thus of the attitude of the papal hierarchy as regards freedom of conscience, and of the perils which especially threaten the United States from the success of her policy:

"There are many who are disposed to attribute any fear of Roman Catholicism in the United States to bigotry or childishness. Such see nothing in the character and attitude of Romanism that is hostile to our free institutions, or find nothing portentous in its growth. Let us, then, first compare some of the fundamental principles of our government with those of the Catholic Church.

"The Constitution of the United States guarantees *liberty of conscience*. Nothing is dearer or more fundamental. Pope Pius IX, in his Encyclical Letter of August 15, 1854, said: 'The absurd and erroneous doctrines or ravings in defense of liberty of conscience are a most pestilential error—a pest, of all others, most to be dreaded in a state.' The same pope, in his Encyclical Letter of December 8, 1864, anathematized 'those who assert the liberty of conscience and of religious worship,' also 'all such as maintain that the church may not employ force.'

"The pacific tone of Rome in the United States does not imply a change of heart. She is tolerant where she is helpless. Says Bishop O'Connor: 'Religious liberty is merely endured until the opposite can be carried into effect without peril to the Catholic world.' ... The archbishop of St. Louis once said: 'Heresy and unbelief are crimes; and in Christian countries, as in Italy and Spain, for instance, where all the people are Catholics, and where the Catholic religion is an essential part of the law of the land, they are punished as other crimes.' ...

"Every cardinal, archbishop, and bishop in the Catholic Church takes an oath of allegiance to the pope, in which occur the following words: 'Heretics, schismatics, and rebels to our said lord (the pope), or his aforesaid successors, I will to my utmost persecute and oppose.' " —Josiah Strong, *Our Country*, ch. 5, pars. 2-4.

It is true that there are real Christians in the Roman Catholic communion. Thousands in that church are serving God according to the best light they have. They are not allowed access to His word, and therefore they do not discern the truth. They have never seen the contrast between a living heart service and a round of mere forms and ceremonies. God looks with pitying tenderness upon these souls, educated as they are in a faith that is delusive and unsatisfying. He will cause rays of light to penetrate the dense darkness that surrounds them. He will reveal to them the truth as it is in Jesus, and many will yet take their position with His people.

But Romanism as a system is no more in harmony with the gospel of Christ now than at any former period in her history. The Protestant churches are in great darkness, or they would discern the signs of the times. The Roman Church is far-reaching in her plans and modes of operation. She is employing every device to extend her influence and increase her power in preparation for a fierce and determined conflict to regain control of the world, to re-establish persecution, and to undo all that Protestantism has done. Catholicism is gaining ground upon every side. See the increasing number of her churches and chapels in Protestant countries. Look at the popularity of her colleges and seminaries in America, so widely patronized by Protestants. Look at the growth of ritualism in England and the frequent defections to the ranks of the Catholics. These things should awaken the anxiety of all who prize the pure principles of the gospel.

Protestants have tampered with and patronized popery; they have made compromises and concessions which papists themselves are surprised to see and fail to understand. Men are closing their eyes to the real character of Romanism and the dangers to be apprehended from her supremacy. The people need to be aroused to resist the advances of this most dangerous foe to civil and religious liberty.

Many Protestants suppose that the Catholic religion is unattractive and that its worship is a dull, meaningless round of ceremony. Here they mistake. While Romanism is based upon deception, it is not a coarse and clumsy imposture. The religious service of the Roman Church is a most impressive ceremonial. Its gorgeous display and solemn rites fascinate the senses of the people and silence the voice of reason and of conscience. The eye is charmed. Magnificent churches, imposing processions, golden altars, jeweled shrines, choice paintings, and exquisite sculpture appeal to the love of beauty. The ear also is captivated. The music is unsurpassed. The rich notes of the deep-toned organ, blending with the melody of many voices as it swells through the lofty domes and pillared aisles of her grand cathedrals, cannot fail to impress the mind with awe and reverence.

This outward splendor, pomp, and ceremony, that only mocks the longings of the sin-sick soul, is an evidence of inward corruption. The religion of Christ needs not such attractions to recommend it. In the light shining from the cross, true Christianity appears so pure and lovely that no external decorations can enhance its true worth. It is the beauty of holiness, a meek and quiet spirit, which is of value with God.

Brilliancy of style is not necessarily an index of pure, elevated thought. High conceptions of art, delicate refinement of taste, often exist in minds that are earthly and sensual. They are often employed by Satan to lead men to forget the necessities of the soul, to lose sight of the future, immortal life, to turn away from their infinite Helper, and to live for this world alone.

A religion of externals is attractive to the unrenewed heart. The pomp and ceremony of the Catholic worship has a seductive, bewitching power, by which many are deceived; and they come to look upon the Roman Church as the very gate of heaven. None but those who have planted their feet firmly upon the foundation of truth, and whose hearts are renewed by the Spirit of God, are proof against her influence. Thousands who have not an experimental knowledge of Christ will be led to accept the forms of godliness without the power. Such a religion is just what the multitudes desire.

The church's claim to the right to pardon leads the Romanist to feel at liberty to sin; and the ordinance of confession, without which her pardon is not granted, tends also to give license to evil. He who kneels before fallen man, and opens in confession the secret thoughts and imaginations of his heart, is debasing his manhood and degrading every noble instinct of his soul. In unfolding the sins of his life to a priest,—an erring, sinful mortal, and too often corrupted with wine and licentiousness,—his standard of character is lowered, and he is defiled in consequence. His thought of God is degraded to the likeness of fallen humanity, for the priest stands as a representative of God. This degrading confession of man to man is the secret spring from which has flowed much of the evil that is defiling the world and fitting it for the final destruction. Yet to him who loves self-indulgence, it is more pleasing to confess to a fellow mortal than to open the soul to God.

It is more palatable to human nature to do penance than to renounce sin; it is easier to mortify the flesh by sackcloth and nettles and galling chains than to crucify fleshly lusts. Heavy is the yoke which the carnal heart is willing to bear rather than bow to the yoke of Christ.

There is a striking similarity between the Church of Rome and the Jewish Church at the time of Christ's first advent. While the Jews secretly trampled upon every principle of the law of God, they were outwardly rigorous in the observance of its precepts, loading it down with exactions and traditions that made obedience painful and burdensome. As the Jews professed to revere the law, so do Romanists claim to reverence the cross. They exalt the symbol of Christ's sufferings, while in their lives they deny Him whom it represents.

Papists place crosses upon their churches, upon their altars, and upon their garments. Everywhere is seen the insignia of the cross. Everywhere it is outwardly honored and exalted. But the teachings of Christ are buried beneath a mass of senseless traditions, false interpretations, and rigorous exactions. The Saviour's words concerning the bigoted Jews, apply with still greater force to the leaders of the Roman Catholic Church: "They bind heavy burdens and grievous to be borne, and lay them on men's shoulders; but they themselves will not move them with one of their fingers." Matthew 23:4. Conscientious souls are kept in constant terror fearing the wrath of an offended God, while many of the dignitaries of the church are living in luxury and sensual pleasure.

The worship of images and relics, the invocation of saints, and the exaltation of the pope are devices of Satan to attract the minds of the people from God and from His Son. To accomplish their ruin, he endeavors to turn their attention from Him through whom alone they can find salvation. He will direct them to any object that can be substituted for the One who has said: "Come unto Me, all ye that labor and are heavy-laden, and I will give you rest." Matthew 11:28.

It is Satan's constant effort to misrepresent the character of God, the nature of sin, and the real issues at stake in the great controversy. His sophistry lessens the obligation of the divine law and gives men license to sin. At the same time he causes them to cherish false conceptions of God so that they regard Him with fear and hate rather than with love. The cruelty inherent in his own character is attributed to the Creator; it is embodied in systems of religion and expressed in modes of worship. Thus the minds of men are blinded, and Satan secures them as his agents to war against God. By perverted conceptions of the divine attributes, heathen nations were led to believe human sacrifices necessary to secure the favor of Deity; and horrible cruelties have been perpetrated under the various forms of idolatry.

The Roman Catholic Church, uniting the forms of paganism and Christianity, and, like paganism, misrepresenting the character of God, has resorted to practices no less cruel and revolting. In the days of Rome's supremacy there were instruments of torture to compel assent to her doctrines. There was the stake for those who would not concede to her claims. There were massacres on a scale that will never be known until revealed in the judgment. Dignitaries of the church studied, under Satan their master, to invent means to cause the greatest possible torture and not end the life of the victim. In many cases the infernal process was repeated to the utmost limit of human endurance, until nature gave up the struggle, and the sufferer hailed death as a sweet release.

Such was the fate of Rome's opponents. For her adherents she had the discipline of the scourge, of famishing hunger, of bodily austerities in every conceivable, heart-sickening form. To secure the favor of Heaven, penitents violated the laws of God by violating the laws of nature. They were taught to sunder the ties which He has formed to bless and gladden man's earthly sojourn. The churchyard contains millions of victims who spent their lives in vain endeavors to subdue their natural affections, to repress, as offensive to God, every thought and feeling of sympathy with their fellow creatures.

If we desire to understand the determined cruelty of Satan, manifested for hundreds of years, not among those who never heard of God, but in the very heart and throughout the extent of Christendom, we have only to look at the history of Romanism. Through this mammoth system of deception the prince of evil achieves his purpose of bringing dishonor to God and wretchedness to man. And as we see how he succeeds in disguising himself and accomplishing his work through the leaders of the church, we may better understand why he has so great antipathy to the Bible. If that Book is read, the mercy and love of God will be revealed; it will be seen that He lays upon men none of these heavy burdens. All that He asks is a broken and contrite heart, a humble, obedient spirit.

Christ gives no example in His life for men and women to shut themselves in monasteries in order to become fitted for heaven. He has never taught that love and sympathy must be repressed. The Saviour's heart overflowed with love. The nearer man approaches to moral perfection, the keener are his sensibilities, the more acute is his perception of sin, and the deeper his sympathy for the afflicted. The pope claims to be the vicar of Christ; but how does his character bear comparison with that of our Saviour? Was Christ ever known to consign men to the prison or the rack because they did not pay Him homage as the King of heaven? Was His voice heard condemning to death those who did not accept Him? When He was slighted by the people of a Samaritan village, the apostle John was filled with indignation, and inquired: "Lord, wilt Thou that we command fire to come down from heaven, and consume them, even as Elias did?" Jesus looked with pity upon His disciple, and rebuked his harsh spirit, saying: "The Son of man is not come to destroy men's lives, but to save them." Luke 9:54, 56. How different from the spirit manifested by Christ is that of His professed vicar.

The Roman Church now presents a fair front to the world, covering with apologies her record of horrible cruelties. She has clothed herself in Christlike garments; but she is unchanged. Every principle of the papacy that existed in past ages exists today. The doctrines devised in the darkest ages are still held. Let none deceive themselves. The papacy that Protestants are now so ready to honor is the same that ruled the world in the days of the Reformation, when men of God stood up, at the peril of their lives, to expose her iniquity. She possesses the same pride and arrogant assumption that lorded it over kings and princes, and claimed the prerogatives of God. Her spirit is no less cruel and despotic now than when she crushed out human liberty and slew the saints of the Most High.

The papacy is just what prophecy declared that she would be, the apostasy of the latter times. 2 Thessalonians 2:3, 4. It is a part of her policy to assume the character which will best accomplish her purpose; but beneath the variable appearance of the chameleon she conceals the invariable venom of the serpent. "Faith ought not to be kept with heretics, nor persons suspected of heresy" (Lenfant, volume 1, page 516), she declares. Shall this power, whose record for a thousand years is written in the blood of the saints, be now acknowledged as a part of the church of Christ?

It is not without reason that the claim has been put forth in Protestant countries that Catholicism differs less widely from Protestantism than in former times. There has been a change; but the change is not in the papacy. Catholicism indeed resembles much of the Protestantism that now exists, because Protestantism has so greatly degenerated since the days of the Reformers.

As the Protestant churches have been seeking the favor of the world, false charity has blinded their eyes. They do not see but that it is right to believe good of all evil, and as the inevitable result they will finally believe evil of all good. Instead of standing in defense of the faith once delivered to the saints, they are now, as it were, apologizing to Rome for their uncharitable opinion of her, begging pardon for their bigotry.

A large class, even of those who look upon Romanism with no favor, apprehend little danger from her power and influence. Many urge that the intellectual and moral darkness prevailing during the Middle Ages favored the spread of her dogmas, superstitions, and oppression, and that the greater intelligence of modern times, the general diffusion of knowledge, and the increasing liberality in matters of religion forbid a revival of intolerance and tyranny. The very thought that such a state of things will exist in this enlightened age is ridiculed. It is true that great light, intellectual, moral, and religious, is shining upon this generation. In the open pages of God's Holy Word, light from heaven has been shed upon the world. But it should be remembered that the greater the light bestowed, the greater the darkness of those who pervert and reject it.

A prayerful study of the Bible would show Protestants the real character of the papacy and would cause them to abhor and to shun it; but many are so wise in their own conceit that they feel no need of humbly seeking God that they may be led into the truth. Although priding themselves on their enlightenment, they are ignorant both of the Scriptures and of the power of God. They must have some means of quieting their consciences, and they seek that which is least spiritual and humiliating. What they desire is a method of forgetting God which shall pass as a method of remembering Him. The papacy is well adapted to meet the wants of all these. It is prepared for two classes of mankind, embracing nearly the whole world—those who would be saved by their merits, and those who would be saved in their sins. Here is the secret of its power.

A day of great intellectual darkness has been shown to be favorable to the success of the papacy. It will yet be demonstrated that a day of great intellectual light is equally favorable for its success. In past ages, when men were without God's word and without the knowledge of the truth, their eyes were blindfolded, and thousands were ensnared, not seeing the net spread for their feet. In this generation there are many whose eyes become dazzled by the glare of human speculations, "science falsely so called;" they discern not the net, and walk into it as readily as if blindfolded. God designed that man's intellectual powers should be held as a gift from his Maker and should be employed in the service of truth and righteousness; but when pride and ambition are cherished, and men exalt their own theories above the word of God, then intelligence can accomplish greater harm than ignorance. Thus the false science of the present day, which undermines faith in the Bible, will prove as successful in preparing the way for the acceptance of the papacy, with its pleasing forms, as did the withholding of knowledge in opening the way for its aggrandizement in the Dark Ages.

In the movements now in progress in the United States to secure for the institutions and usages of the church the support of the state, Protestants are following in the steps of papists. Nay, more, they are opening the door for the papacy to regain in Protestant America the supremacy which she has lost in the Old World. And that which gives greater significance to this movement is the fact that the principal object contemplated is the enforcement of Sunday observance—a custom which originated with Rome, and which she claims as the sign of her authority. It is the spirit of the papacy—the spirit of conformity to worldly customs, the veneration for human traditions above the commandments of God—that is permeating the Protestant churches and leading them on to do the same work of Sunday exaltation which the papacy has done before them.

If the reader would understand the agencies to be employed in the soon-coming contest, he has but to trace the record of the means which Rome employed for the same object in ages past. If he would know how papists and Protestants united will deal with those who reject their dogmas, let him see the spirit which Rome manifested toward the Sabbath and its defenders.

Royal edicts, general councils, and church ordinances sustained by secular power were the steps by which the pagan festival attained its position of honor in the Christian world. The first public measure enforcing Sunday observance was the law enacted by Constantine. (A.D. 321) This edict required townspeople to rest on "the venerable day of the sun," but permitted countrymen to continue their agricultural pursuits. Though virtually a heathen statute, it was enforced by the emperor after his nominal acceptance of Christianity.

The royal mandate not proving a sufficient substitute for divine authority, Eusebius, a bishop who sought the favor of princes, and who was the special friend and flatterer of Constantine, advanced the claim that Christ had transferred the Sabbath to Sunday. Not a single testimony of the Scriptures was produced in proof of the new doctrine. Eusebius himself unwittingly acknowledges its falsity and points to the real authors of the change. "All things," he says, "whatever that it was duty to do on the Sabbath, these we have transferred to the Lord's Day."—Robert Cox, *Sabbath Laws and Sabbath Duties*, page 538. But the Sunday argument, groundless as it was, served to embolden men in trampling upon the Sabbath of the Lord. All who desired to be honored by the world accepted the popular festival.

As the papacy became firmly established, the work of Sunday exaltation was continued. For a time the people engaged in agricultural labor when not attending church, and the seventh day was still regarded as the Sabbath. But steadily a change was effected. Those in holy office were forbidden to pass judgment in any civil controversy on the Sunday. Soon after, all persons, of whatever rank, were commanded to refrain from common labor on pain of a fine for freemen and stripes in the case of servants. Later it was decreed that rich men should be punished with the loss of half of their estates; and finally, that if still obstinate they should be made slaves. The lower classes were to suffer perpetual banishment.

Miracles also were called into requisition. Among other wonders it was reported that as a husbandman who was about to plow his field on Sunday cleaned his plow with an iron, the iron stuck fast in his hand, and for two years he carried it about with him, "to his exceeding great pain and shame."—Francis West, *Historical and Practical Discourse on the Lord's Day*, page 174.

Later the pope gave directions that the parish priest should admonish the violators of Sunday and wish them to go to church and say their prayers, lest they bring some great calamity on themselves and neighbors. An ecclesiastical council brought forward the argument, since so widely employed, even by Protestants, that because persons had been struck by lightning while laboring on Sunday, it must be the

Sabbath. "It is apparent," said the prelates, "how high the displeasure of God was upon their neglect of this day." An appeal was then made that priests and ministers, kings and princes, and all faithful people "use their utmost endeavors and care that the day be restored to its honor, and, for the credit of Christianity, more devoutly observed for the time to come."—Thomas Morer, *Discourse in Six Dialogues on the Name, Notion, and Observation of the Lord's Day*, page 271.

The decrees of councils proving insufficient, the secular authorities were besought to issue an edict that would strike terror to the hearts of the people and force them to refrain from labor on the Sunday. At a synod held in Rome, all previous decisions were reaffirmed with greater force and solemnity. They were also incorporated into the ecclesiastical law and enforced by the civil authorities throughout nearly all Christendom. (See Heylyn, *History of the Sabbath*, pt. 2, ch. 5, sec. 7.)

Still the absence of Scriptural authority for Sundaykeeping occasioned no little embarrassment. The people questioned the right of their teachers to set aside the positive declaration of Jehovah, "The seventh day is the Sabbath of the Lord thy God," in order to honor the day of the sun. To supply the lack of Bible testimony, other expedients were necessary. A zealous advocate of Sunday, who about the close of the twelfth century visited the churches of England, was resisted by faithful witnesses for the truth; and so fruitless were his efforts that he departed from the country for a season and cast about him for some means to enforce his teachings. When he returned, the lack was supplied, and in his after labors he met with greater success. He brought with him a roll purporting to be from God Himself, which contained the needed command for Sunday observance, with awful threats to terrify the disobedient. This precious document—as base a counterfeit as the institution it supported—was said to have fallen from heaven and to have been found in Jerusalem, upon the altar of St. Simeon, in Golgotha. But, in fact, the pontifical palace at Rome was the source whence it proceeded. Frauds and forgeries to advance the power and prosperity of the church have in all ages been esteemed lawful by the papal hierarchy.

The roll forbade labor from the ninth hour, three o'clock, on Saturday afternoon, till sunrise on Monday; and its authority was declared to be confirmed by many miracles. It was reported that persons laboring beyond the appointed hour were stricken with paralysis. A miller who attempted to grind his corn, saw, instead of flour, a torrent of blood come forth, and the mill wheel stood still, notwithstanding the strong rush of water. A woman who placed dough in the oven found it raw when taken out, though the oven was very hot. Another who had dough prepared for baking at the ninth hour, but determined to set it aside till Monday, found, the next day, that it had been made into loaves and baked by divine power. A man who baked bread after the ninth hour on Saturday found, when he broke it the next morning, that blood started therefrom. By such absurd and superstitious fabrications did the advocates of Sunday endeavor to establish its sacredness. (See Roger de Hoveden, *Annals*, vol. 2, pp. 528-530.)

In Scotland, as in England, a greater regard for Sunday was secured by uniting with it a portion of the ancient Sabbath. But the time required to be kept holy varied. An edict from the king of Scotland declared that "Saturday from twelve at noon ought to be accounted holy," and that no man, from that time till Monday morning, should engage in worldly business.—Morer, pages 290, 291.

But notwithstanding all the efforts to establish Sunday sacredness, papists themselves publicly confessed the divine authority of the Sabbath and the human origin of the institution by which it had been supplanted. In the sixteenth century a papal council plainly declared: "Let all Christians remember that the seventh day was consecrated by God, and hath been received and observed, not only by the Jews, but by all others who pretend to worship God; though we Christians have changed their Sabbath into the Lord's Day."—*Ibid*., pages 281, 282. Those who were tampering with the divine law were not ignorant of the character of their work. They were deliberately setting themselves above God.

A striking illustration of Rome's policy toward those who disagree with her was given in the long and bloody persecution of the Waldenses, some of whom were observers of the Sabbath. Others suffered in a similar manner for their fidelity to the fourth commandment. The history of the churches of Ethiopia and Abyssinia is especially significant. Amid the gloom of the Dark Ages, the Christians of Central Africa were lost sight of and forgotten by the world, and for many centuries they enjoyed freedom in the exercise of their faith. But at last Rome learned of their existence, and the emperor of Abyssinia was soon beguiled into an acknowledgment of the pope as the vicar of Christ. Other concessions followed. An edict was issued forbidding the observance of the Sabbath under the severest penalties. (See Michael Geddes, *Church History of Ethiopia*, pages 311, 312.) But papal tyranny soon became a yoke so galling that the Abyssinians determined to break it from their necks. After a terrible struggle the Romanists were banished from their dominions, and the ancient faith was restored. The churches rejoiced in their freedom, and they never forgot the lesson they had learned concerning the deception, the fanaticism, and the despotic power of Rome. Within their solitary realm they were content to remain, unknown to the rest of Christendom.

The churches of Africa held the Sabbath as it was held by the papal church before her complete apostasy. While they kept the seventh day in obedience to the commandment of God, they abstained from labor on the Sunday in conformity to the custom of the church. Upon obtaining supreme power, Rome had trampled upon the Sabbath of God to exalt her own; but the churches of Africa, hidden for nearly a thousand years, did not share in this apostasy. When brought under the sway of Rome, they were forced to set aside the true and exalt the false sabbath; but no sooner had they regained their independence than they returned to obedience to the fourth commandment.

These records of the past clearly reveal the enmity of Rome toward the true Sabbath and its defenders, and the means which she employs to honor the institution of her creating. The word of God teaches that these scenes are to be repeated as Roman Catholics and Protestants shall unite for the exaltation of the Sunday.

The prophecy of Revelation 13 declares that the power represented by the beast with lamblike horns shall cause "the earth and them which dwell therein" to worship the papacy—there symbolized by the beast "like unto a leopard." The beast with two horns is also to say "to them that dwell on the earth, that they should make an image to the beast;" and, furthermore, it is to command all, "both small and great, rich and poor, free and bond," to receive the mark of the beast. Revelation 13:11-16. It has been shown that the United States is the power represented by the beast with lamblike horns, and that this prophecy will be fulfilled when the United States shall enforce Sunday observance, which Rome claims as the special acknowledgment of her supremacy. But in this homage to the papacy the United States will not be alone. The influence of Rome in the countries that once acknowledged her dominion is still far from being destroyed. And prophecy foretells a restoration of her power. "I saw one of his heads as it were wounded to death; and his deadly wound was healed: and all the world wondered after the beast." Verse 3. The infliction of the deadly wound points to the downfall of the papacy in 1798. After this, says the prophet, "his deadly wound was healed: and all the world wondered after the beast." Paul states plainly that the "man of sin" will continue until the second advent. 2 Thessalonians 2:3-8. To the very close of time he will carry forward the work of deception. And the revelator declares, also referring to the papacy: "All that dwell upon the earth shall worship him, whose names are not written in the book of life." Revelation 13:8. In both the Old and the New World, the papacy will receive homage in the honor paid to the Sunday institution, that rests solely upon the authority of the Roman Church.

Since the middle of the nineteenth century, students of prophecy in the United States have presented this testimony to the world. In the events now taking place is seen a rapid advance toward the fulfillment of the prediction. With Protestant teachers there is the same claim of divine authority for Sundaykeeping, and the same lack of Scriptural evidence, as with the papal leaders who fabricated miracles to supply the place of a command from God. The assertion that God's judgments are visited upon men for their violation of the Sunday-sabbath, will be repeated; already it is beginning to be urged. And a movement to enforce Sunday observance is fast gaining ground.

Marvelous in her shrewdness and cunning is the Roman Church. She can read what is to be. She bides her time, seeing that the Protestant churches are paying her homage in their acceptance of the false sabbath and that they are preparing to enforce it by the very means which she herself employed in bygone days. Those who reject the light of truth will yet seek the aid of this self-styled infallible power to exalt an institution that originated with her. How readily she will come to the help of Protestants in this work it is not difficult to conjecture. Who understands better than the papal leaders how to deal with those who are disobedient to the church?

The Roman Catholic Church, with all its ramifications throughout the world, forms one vast organization under the control, and designed to serve the interests, of the papal see. Its millions of communicants, in every country on the globe, are instructed to hold themselves as bound in allegiance to the pope. Whatever their nationality or their government, they are to regard the authority of the church as above all other. Though they may take the oath pledging their loyalty to the state, yet back of this lies the vow of obedience to Rome, absolving them from every pledge inimical to her interests.

History testifies of her artful and persistent efforts to insinuate herself into the affairs of nations; and having gained a foothold, to further her own aims, even at the ruin of princes and people. In the year 1204, Pope Innocent III extracted from Peter II, king of Arragon, the following extraordinary oath: "I, Peter, king of Arragonians, profess and promise to be ever faithful and obedient to my lord, Pope Innocent, to his Catholic successors, and the Roman Church, and faithfully to preserve my kingdom in his obedience, defending the Catholic faith, and persecuting heretical pravity."—John Dowling, *The History of Romanism*, b. 5, ch. 6, sec. 55. This is in harmony with the claims regarding the power of the Roman pontiff "that it is lawful for him to depose emperors" and "that he can absolve subjects from their allegiance to unrighteous rulers."—Mosheim, b. 3, cent. 11, pt. 2, ch. 2, sec. 9, note 17.

And let it be remembered, it is the boast of Rome that she never changes. The principles of Gregory VII and Innocent III are still the principles of the Roman Catholic Church. And had she but the power, she would put them in practice with as much vigor now as in past centuries. Protestants little know what they are doing when they propose to accept the aid of Rome in the work of Sunday exaltation. While they are bent upon the accomplishment of their purpose, Rome is aiming to re-establish her power, to recover her lost supremacy. Let the principle once be established in the United States that the church may employ or control the power of the state; that religious observances may be enforced by secular laws; in short, that the authority of church and state is to dominate the conscience, and the triumph of Rome in this country is assured.

God's word has given warning of the impending danger; let this be unheeded, and the Protestant world will learn what the purposes of Rome really are, only when it is too late to escape the snare. She is silently growing into power. Her doctrines are exerting their influence in legislative halls, in the churches, and in the hearts of men. She is piling up her lofty and massive structures in the secret recesses of which her former persecutions will be repeated. Stealthily and unsuspectedly she is strengthening her forces to further her own ends when the time shall come for her to strike. All that she desires is vantage ground, and this is already being given her. We shall soon see and shall feel what the purpose of the Roman element is. Whoever shall believe and obey the word of God will thereby incur reproach and persecution.

Ten

—The Impending Conflict—

From the very beginning of the great controversy in heaven it has been Satan's purpose to overthrow the law of God. It was to accomplish this that he entered upon his rebellion against the Creator, and though he was cast out of heaven he has continued the same warfare upon the earth. To deceive men, and thus lead them to transgress God's law, is the object which he has steadfastly pursued. Whether this be accomplished by casting aside the law altogether, or by rejecting one of its precepts, the result will be ultimately the same. He that offends "in one point," manifests contempt for the whole law; his influence and example are on the side of transgression; he becomes "guilty of all." James 2:10.

In seeking to cast contempt upon the divine statutes, Satan has perverted the doctrines of the Bible, and errors have thus become incorporated into the faith of thousands who profess to believe the Scriptures. The last great conflict between truth and error is but the final struggle of the long-standing controversy concerning the law of God. Upon this battle we are now entering—a battle between the laws of men and the precepts of Jehovah, between the religion of the Bible and the religion of fable and tradition.

The agencies which will unite against truth and righteousness in this contest are now actively at work. God's holy word, which has been handed down to us at such a cost of suffering and blood, is but little valued. The Bible is within the reach of all, but there are few who really accept it as the guide of life. Infidelity prevails to an alarming extent, not in the world merely, but in the church. Many have come to deny doctrines which are the very pillars of the Christian faith. The great facts of creation as presented by the inspired writers, the fall of man, the atonement, and the perpetuity of the law of God, are practically rejected, either wholly or in part, by a large share of the professedly Christian world. Thousands who pride themselves upon their wisdom and independence regard it as an evidence of weakness to place implicit confidence in the Bible; they think it a proof of superior talent and learning to cavil at the Scriptures and to spiritualize and explain away their most important truths. Many ministers are teaching their people, and many professors and teachers are instructing their students, that the law of God has been changed or abrogated; and those who regard its requirements as still valid, to be literally obeyed, are thought to be deserving only of ridicule or contempt.

In rejecting the truth, men reject its Author. In trampling upon the law of God, they deny the authority of the Law-giver. It is as easy to make an idol of false doctrines and theories as to fashion an idol of wood or stone. By misrepresenting the attributes of God, Satan leads men to conceive of Him in a false character. With many, a philosophical idol is enthroned in the place of Jehovah; while the living God, as He is revealed in His word, in Christ, and in the works of creation, is worshiped by but few. Thousands deify nature while they deny the God of nature. Though in a different form, idolatry exists in the Christian world today as verily as it existed among ancient Israel in the days of Elijah. The god of many professedly wise men, of philosophers, poets, politicians, journalists—the god of polished fashionable circles, of many colleges and universities, even of some theological institutions—is little better than Baal, the sun-god of Phoenicia.

No error accepted by the Christian world strikes more boldly against the authority of Heaven, none is more directly opposed to the dictates of reason, none is more pernicious in its results, than the modern doctrine, so rapidly gaining ground, that God's law is no longer binding upon men. Every nation has its laws, which command respect and obedience; no government could exist without them; and can it be conceived that the Creator of the heavens and the earth has no law to govern the beings He has made? Suppose that prominent ministers were publicly to teach that the statutes which govern their land and protect the rights of its citizens were not obligatory—that they restricted the liberties of the people, and therefore ought not to be obeyed; how long would such men be tolerated in the pulpit? But is it a graver offense to disregard the laws of states and nations than to trample upon those divine precepts which are the foundation of all government?

It would be far more consistent for nations to abolish their statutes, and permit the people to do as they please, than for the Ruler of the universe to annul His law, and leave the world without a standard to condemn the guilty or justify the obedient. Would we know the result of making void the law of God? The experiment has been tried. Terrible were the scenes enacted in France when atheism became the controlling power. It was then demonstrated to the world that to throw off the restraints which God has imposed is to accept the rule of the cruelest of tyrants. When the standard of righteousness is set aside, the way is open for the prince of evil to establish his power in the earth.

Wherever the divine precepts are rejected, sin ceases to appear sinful or righteousness desirable. Those who refuse to submit to the government of God are wholly unfitted to govern themselves. Through their pernicious teachings the spirit of insubordination is implanted in the hearts of children and youth, who are naturally impatient of control; and a lawless, licentious state of society results. While scoffing at the credulity of those who obey the requirements of God, the multitudes eagerly accept the delusions of Satan. They give the rein to lust and practice the sins which have called down judgments upon the heathen.

Those who teach the people to regard lightly the commandments of God sow disobedience to reap disobedience. Let the restraint imposed by the divine law be wholly cast aside, and human laws would soon be disregarded. Because God forbids dishonest practices, coveting, lying, and defrauding, men are ready to trample upon His statutes as a hindrance to their worldly prosperity; but the results of banishing these precepts would be such as they do not anticipate. If the law were not binding, why should any fear to transgress? Property would no longer be safe. Men would obtain their neighbor's possessions by violence, and the strongest would become richest. Life itself would not be respected. The marriage vow would no longer stand as a sacred bulwark to protect the family. He who had the power, would, if he desired, take his neighbor's wife by violence. The fifth commandment would be set aside with the fourth. Children would not shrink from taking the life of their parents if by so doing they could obtain the desire of their corrupt hearts. The civilized world would become a horde of robbers and assassins; and peace, rest, and happiness would be banished from the earth.

Already the doctrine that men are released from obedience to God's requirements has weakened the force of moral obligation and opened the floodgates of iniquity upon the world. Lawlessness, dissipation, and corruption are sweeping in upon us like an overwhelming tide. In the family, Satan is at work. His banner waves, even in professedly Christian households. There is envy, evil surmising, hypocrisy, estrangement, emulation, strife, betrayal of sacred trusts, indulgence of lust. The whole system of religious principles and doctrines, which should form the foundation and framework of social life, seems to be a tottering mass, ready to fall to ruin. The vilest of criminals, when thrown into prison for their offenses, are often made the recipients of gifts and attentions as if they had attained an enviable distinction. Great publicity is given to their character and crimes. The press publishes the revolting details of vice, thus initiating others into the practice of fraud, robbery, and murder; and Satan exults in the success of his hellish schemes. The infatuation of vice, the wanton taking of life, the terrible increase of intemperance and iniquity of every order and degree, should arouse all who fear God, to inquire what can be done to stay the tide of evil.

Courts of justice are corrupt. Rulers are actuated by desire for gain and love of sensual pleasure. Intemperance has beclouded the faculties of many so that Satan has almost complete control of them. Jurists are perverted, bribed, deluded. Drunkenness and revelry, passion, envy, dishonesty of every sort, are represented among those who administer the laws. "Justice standeth afar off: for truth is fallen in the street, and equity cannot enter." Isaiah 59:14.

The iniquity and spiritual darkness that prevailed under the supremacy of Rome were the inevitable result of her suppression of the Scriptures; but where is to be found the cause of the widespread infidelity, the rejection of the law of God, and the consequent corruption, under the full blaze of gospel light in an age of religious freedom? Now that Satan can no longer keep the world under his control by withholding the Scriptures, he resorts to other means to accomplish the same object. To destroy faith in the Bible serves his purpose as well as to destroy the Bible itself. By introducing the belief that God's law is not binding, he as effectually leads men to transgress as if they were wholly ignorant of its precepts. And now, as in former ages, he has worked through the church to further his designs. The religious organizations of the day have refused to listen to unpopular truths plainly brought to view in the Scriptures, and in combating them they have adopted interpretations and taken positions which have sown broadcast the seeds of skepticism. Clinging to the papal error of natural immortality and man's consciousness in death, they have rejected the only defense against the delusions of spiritualism. The doctrine of eternal torment has led many to disbelieve the Bible. And as the claims of the fourth commandment are urged upon the people, it is found that the observance of the seventh-day Sabbath is enjoined; and as the only way to free themselves from a duty which they are unwilling to perform, many popular teachers declare that the law of God is no longer binding. Thus they cast away the law and the Sabbath together. As the work of Sabbath reform extends, this rejection of the divine law to avoid the claims of the fourth commandment will become well-nigh universal. The teachings of religious leaders have opened the door to infidelity, to spiritualism, and to contempt for God's holy law; and upon these leaders rests a fearful responsibility for the iniquity that exists in the Christian world.

Yet this very class put forth the claim that the fast-spreading corruption is largely attributable to the desecration of the so called "Christian sabbath," and that the enforcement of Sunday observance would greatly improve the morals of society. This claim is especially urged in America, where the doctrine of the true Sabbath has been most widely preached. Here the temperance work, one of the most prominent and important of moral reforms, is often combined with the Sunday movement, and the advocates of the latter represent themselves as laboring to promote the highest interest of society; and those who refuse to unite with them are denounced as the enemies of temperance and reform. But the fact that a movement to establish error is connected with a work which is in itself good, is not an argument in favor of the error. We may disguise poison by mingling it with wholesome food, but we do not change its nature. On the contrary, it is rendered more dangerous, as it is more likely to be taken unawares. It is one of Satan's devices to combine with falsehood just enough truth to give it plausibility. The leaders of the Sunday movement may advocate reforms which the people need, principles which are in harmony with the Bible; yet while there is with these a requirement which is contrary to God's law, His servants cannot unite with them. Nothing can justify them in setting aside the commandments of God for the precepts of men.

Through the two great errors, the immortality of the soul and Sunday sacredness, Satan will bring the people under his deceptions.

While the former lays the foundation of spiritualism, the latter creates a bond of sympathy with Rome. The Protestants of the United States will be foremost in stretching their hands across the gulf to grasp the hand of spiritualism; they will reach over the abyss to clasp hands with the Roman power; and under the influence of this threefold union, this country will follow in the steps of Rome in trampling on the rights of conscience.

As spiritualism more closely imitates the nominal Christianity of the day, it has greater power to deceive and ensnare. Satan himself is converted, after the modern order of things. He will appear in the character of an angel of light. Through the agency of spiritualism, miracles will be wrought, the sick will be healed, and many undeniable wonders will be performed. And as the spirits will profess faith in the Bible, and manifest respect for the institutions of the church, their work will be accepted as a manifestation of divine power.

The line of distinction between professed Christians and the ungodly is now hardly distinguishable. Church members love what the world loves and are ready to join with them, and Satan determines to unite them in one body and thus strengthen his cause by sweeping all into the ranks of spiritualism. Papists, who boast of miracles as a certain sign of the true church, will be readily deceived by this wonder-working power; and Protestants, having cast away the shield of truth, will also be deluded. Papists, Protestants, and worldlings will alike accept the form of godliness without the power, and they will see in this union a grand movement for the conversion of the world and the ushering in of the long-expected millennium.

Through spiritualism, Satan appears as a benefactor of the race, healing the diseases of the people, and professing to present a new and more exalted system of religious faith; but at the same time he works as a destroyer. His temptations are leading multitudes to ruin. Intemperance dethrones reason; sensual indulgence, strife, and bloodshed follow. Satan delights in war, for it excites the worst passions of the soul and then sweeps into eternity its victims steeped in vice and blood. It is his object to incite the nations to war against one another, for he can thus divert the minds of the people from the work of preparation to stand in the day of God.

Satan works through the elements also to garner his harvest of unprepared souls. He has studied the secrets of the laboratories of nature, and he uses all his power to control the elements as far as God allows. When he was suffered to afflict Job, how quickly flocks and herds, servants, houses, children, were swept away, one trouble succeeding another as in a moment. It is God that shields His creatures and hedges them in from the power of the destroyer. But the Christian world have shown contempt for the law of Jehovah; and the Lord will do just what He has declared that He would—He will withdraw His blessings from the earth and remove His protecting care from those who are rebelling against His law and teaching and forcing others to do the same. Satan has control of all whom God does not especially guard. He will favor and prosper some in order to further his own designs, and he will bring trouble upon others and lead men to believe that it is God who is afflicting them.

While appearing to the children of men as a great physician who can heal all their maladies, he will bring disease and disaster, until populous cities are reduced to ruin and desolation. Even now he is at work. In accidents and calamities by sea and by land, in great conflagrations, in fierce tornadoes and terrific hailstorms, in tempests, floods, cyclones, tidal waves, and earthquakes, in every place and in a thousand forms, Satan is exercising his power. He sweeps away the ripening harvest, and famine and distress follow. He imparts to the air a deadly taint, and thousands perish by the pestilence. These visitations are to become more and more frequent and disastrous. Destruction will be upon both man and beast. "The earth mourneth and fadeth away," "the haughty people ... do languish. The earth also is defiled under the inhabitants thereof; because they have transgressed the laws, changed the ordinance, broken the everlasting covenant." Isaiah 24:4, 5.

And then the great deceiver will persuade men that those who serve God are causing these evils. The class that have provoked the displeasure of Heaven will charge all their troubles upon those whose obedience to God's commandments is a perpetual reproof to transgressors. It will be declared that men are offending God by the violation of the Sunday sabbath; that this sin has brought calamities which will not cease until Sunday observance shall be strictly enforced; and that those who present the claims of the fourth commandment, thus destroying reverence for Sunday, are troublers of the people, preventing their restoration to divine favor and temporal prosperity. Thus the accusation urged of old against the servant of God will be repeated and upon grounds equally well established: "And it came to pass, when Ahab saw Elijah, that Ahab said unto him, Art thou he that troubleth Israel? And he answered, I have not troubled Israel; but thou, and thy father's house, in that ye have forsaken the commandments of the Lord, and thou hast followed Baalim." 1 Kings 18:17, 18. As the wrath of the people shall be excited by false charges, they will pursue a course toward God's ambassadors very similar to that which apostate Israel pursued toward Elijah.

The miracle-working power manifested through spiritualism will exert its influence against those who choose to obey God rather than men. Communications from the spirits will declare that God has sent them to convince the rejecters of Sunday of their error, affirming that the laws of the land should be obeyed as the law of God. They will lament the great wickedness in the world and second the testimony of religious teachers that the degraded state of morals is caused by the desecration of Sunday. Great will be the indignation excited against all who refuse to accept their testimony.

Satan's policy in this final conflict with God's people is the same that he employed in the opening of the great controversy in heaven. He professed to be seeking to promote the stability of the divine government, while secretly bending every effort to secure its overthrow. And the very work which he was thus endeavoring to accomplish he charged upon the loyal angels. The same policy of deception has marked the history of the Roman Church. It has professed to act as the vicegerent of Heaven, while seeking to exalt itself above God and to change His law. Under the rule of Rome, those who suffered death for their fidelity to the gospel were denounced as evildoers; they were declared to be in league with Satan; and every possible means was employed to cover them with reproach, to cause them to appear in the eyes of the people and even to themselves as the vilest of criminals. So it will be now. While Satan seeks to destroy those who honor God's law, he will cause them to be accused as lawbreakers, as men who are dishonoring God and bringing judgments upon the world.

God never forces the will or the conscience; but Satan's constant resort—to gain control of those whom he cannot otherwise seduce—is compulsion by cruelty. Through fear or force he endeavors to rule the conscience and to secure homage to himself. To accomplish this, he works through both religious and secular authorities, moving them to the enforcement of human laws in defiance of the law of God.

Those who honor the Bible Sabbath will be denounced as enemies of law and order, as breaking down the moral restraints of society, causing anarchy and corruption, and calling down the judgments of God upon the earth. Their conscientious scruples will be pronounced obstinacy, stubbornness, and contempt of authority. They will be accused of disaffection toward the government. Ministers who deny the obligation of the divine law will present from the pulpit the duty of yielding obedience to the civil authorities as ordained of God. In legislative halls and courts of justice, commandment keepers will be misrepresented and condemned. A false coloring will be given to their words; the worst construction will be put upon their motives.

As the Protestant churches reject the clear, Scriptural arguments in defense of God's law, they will long to silence those whose faith they cannot overthrow by the Bible. Though they blind their own eyes to the fact, they are now adopting a course which will lead to the persecution of those who conscientiously refuse to do what the rest of the Christian world are doing, and acknowledge the claims of the papal sabbath.

The dignitaries of church and state will unite to bribe, persuade, or compel all classes to honor the Sunday. The lack of divine authority will be supplied by oppressive enactments. Political corruption is destroying love of justice and regard for truth; and even in free America, rulers and legislators, in order to secure public favor, will yield to the popular demand for a law enforcing Sunday observance. Liberty of conscience, which has cost so great a sacrifice, will no longer be respected. In the soon-coming conflict we shall see exemplified the prophet's words: "The dragon was wroth with the woman, and went to make war with the remnant of her seed, which keep the commandments of God, and have the testimony of Jesus Christ." Revelation 12:17.

Eleven

—Modern Revivals—

W herever the word of God has been faithfully preached, results have followed that attested its divine origin. The Spirit of God accompanied the message of His servants, and the word was with power. Sinners felt their consciences quickened. The "light which lighteth every man that cometh into the world" illumined the secret chambers of their souls, and the hidden things of darkness were made manifest. Deep conviction took hold upon their minds and hearts. They were convinced of sin and of righteousness and of judgment to come. They had a sense of the righteousness of Jehovah and felt the terror of appearing, in their guilt and uncleanness, before the Searcher of hearts. In anguish they cried out: "Who shall deliver me from the body of this death?" As the cross of Calvary, with its infinite sacrifice for the sins of men, was revealed, they saw that nothing but the merits of Christ could suffice to atone for their transgressions; this alone could reconcile man to God. With faith and humility they accepted the Lamb of God, that taketh away the sin of the world. Through the blood of Jesus they had "remission of sins that are past."

These souls brought forth fruit meet for repentance. They believed and were baptized, and rose to walk in newness of life—new creatures in Christ Jesus; not to fashion themselves according to the former lusts, but by the faith of the Son of God to follow in His steps, to reflect His character, and to purify themselves even as He is pure. The things they once hated they now loved, and the things they once loved they hated. The proud and self-assertive became meek and lowly of heart. The vain and supercilious became serious and unobtrusive. The profane became reverent, the drunken sober, and the profligate pure. The vain fashions of the world were laid aside. Christians sought not the "outward adorning of plaiting the hair, and of wearing of gold, or of putting on of apparel;

but ... the hidden man of the heart, in that which is not corruptible, even the ornament of a meek and quiet spirit, which is in the sight of God of great price." 1 Peter 3:3, 4.

Revivals brought deep heart-searching and humility. They were characterized by solemn, earnest appeals to the sinner, by yearning compassion for the purchase of the blood of Christ. Men and women prayed and wrestled with God for the salvation of souls. The fruits of such revivals were seen in souls who shrank not at self-denial and sacrifice, but rejoiced that they were counted worthy to suffer reproach and trial for the sake of Christ. Men beheld a transformation in the lives of those who had professed the name of Jesus. The community was benefited by their influence. They gathered with Christ, and sowed to the Spirit, to reap life everlasting.

It could be said of them: "Ye sorrowed to repentance." "For godly sorrow worketh repentance to salvation not to be repented of: but the sorrow of the world worketh death. For behold this selfsame thing, that ye sorrowed after a godly sort, what carefulness it wrought in you, yea, what clearing of yourselves, yea, what indignation, yea, what fear, yea, what vehement desire, yea, what zeal, yea, what revenge! In all things ye have approved yourselves to be clear in this matter." 2 Corinthians 7:9-11.

This is the result of the work of the Spirit of God. There is no evidence of genuine repentance unless it works reformation. If he restore the pledge, give again that he had robbed, confess his sins, and love God and his fellow men, the sinner may be sure that he has found peace with God. Such were the effects that in former years followed seasons of religious awakening. Judged by their fruits, they were known to be blessed of God in the salvation of men and the uplifting of humanity.

But many of the revivals of modern times have presented a marked contrast to those manifestations of divine grace which in earlier days followed the labors of God's servants. It is true that a widespread interest is kindled, many profess conversion, and there are large accessions to the churches; nevertheless the results are not such as to warrant the belief that there has been a corresponding increase of real spiritual life. The light which flames up for a time soon dies out, leaving the darkness more dense than before.

Popular revivals are too often carried by appeals to the imagination, by exciting the emotions, by gratifying the love for what is new and startling. Converts thus gained have little desire to listen to Bible truth, little interest in the testimony of prophets and apostles. Unless a religious service has something of a sensational character, it has no attractions for them. A message which appeals to unimpassioned reason awakens no response. The plain warnings of God's word, relating directly to their eternal interests, are unheeded.

With every truly converted soul the relation to God and to eternal things will be the great topic of life. But where, in the popular churches of today, is the spirit of consecration to God? The converts do not renounce their pride and love of the world. They are no more willing to deny self, to take up the cross, and follow the meek and lowly Jesus, than before their conversion. Religion has become the sport of infidels and skeptics because so many who bear its name are ignorant of its principles. The power of godliness has well-nigh departed from many of the churches. Picnics, church theatricals, church fairs, fine houses, personal display, have banished thoughts of God. Lands and goods and worldly occupations engross the mind, and things of eternal interest receive hardly a passing notice.

Notwithstanding the widespread declension of faith and piety, there are true followers of Christ in these churches. Before the final visitation of God's judgments upon the earth there will be among the people of the Lord such a revival of primitive godliness as has not been witnessed since apostolic times. The Spirit and power of God will be poured out upon His children. At that time many will separate themselves from those churches in which the love of this world has supplanted love for God and His word. Many, both of ministers and people, will gladly accept those great truths which God has caused to be proclaimed at this time to prepare a people for the Lord's second coming. The enemy of souls desires to hinder this work; and before the time for such a movement shall come, he will endeavor to prevent it by introducing a counterfeit. In those churches which he can bring under his deceptive power he will make it appear that God's special blessing is poured out; there will be manifest what is thought to be great religious interest. Multitudes will exult that God is working marvelously for them, when the work is that of another spirit. Under a religious guise, Satan will seek to extend his influence over the Christian world.

In many of the revivals which have occurred during the last half century, the same influences have been at work, to a greater or less degree, that will be manifest in the more extensive movements of the future. There is an emotional excitement, a mingling of the true with the false, that is well adapted to mislead. Yet none need be deceived. In the light of God's word it is not difficult to determine the nature of these movements. Wherever men neglect the testimony of the Bible, turning away from those plain, soul-testing truths which require self-denial and renunciation of the world, there we may be sure that God's blessing is not bestowed. And by the rule which Christ Himself has given, "Ye shall know them by their fruits" (Matthew 7:16), it is evident that these movements are not the work of the Spirit of God.

In the truths of His word, God has given to men a revelation of Himself; and to all who accept them they are a shield against the deceptions of Satan. It is a neglect of these truths that has opened the door to the evils which are now becoming so widespread in the religious world. The nature and the importance of the law of God have been, to a great extent, lost sight of. A wrong conception of the character, the perpetuity, and the obligation of the divine law has led to errors in relation to conversion and sanctification, and has resulted in lowering the standard of piety in the church. Here is to be found the secret of the lack of the Spirit and power of God in the revivals of our time.

There are, in the various denominations, men eminent for their piety, by whom this fact is acknowledged and deplored. Professor Edwards A. Park, in setting forth the current religious perils, ably says: "One source of danger is the neglect of the pulpit to enforce the divine law. In former days the pulpit was an echo of the voice of conscience. … Our most illustrious preachers gave a wonderful majesty to their discourses by following the example of the Master, and giving prominence to the law, its precepts, and its threatenings. They repeated the two great maxims, that the law is a transcript of the divine perfections, and that a man who does not love the law does not love the gospel; for the law, as well as the gospel, is a mirror reflecting the true character of God. This peril leads to another, that of underrating the evil of sin, the extent of it, the demerit of it. In proportion to the rightfulness of the commandment is the wrongfulness of disobeying it. …

"Affiliated to the dangers already named is the danger of underestimating the justice of God. The tendency of the modern pulpit is to strain out the divine justice from the divine benevolence, to sink benevolence into a sentiment rather than exalt it into a principle. The new theological prism puts asunder what God has joined together. Is the divine law a good or an evil? It is a good. Then justice is good; for it is a disposition to execute the law. From the habit of underrating the divine law and justice, the extent and demerit of human disobedience, men easily slide into the habit of underestimating the grace which has provided an atonement for sin." Thus the gospel loses its value and importance in the minds of men, and soon they are ready practically to cast aside the Bible itself.

Many religious teachers assert that Christ by His death abolished the law, and men are henceforth free from its requirements. There are some who represent it as a grievous yoke, and in contrast to the bondage of the law they present the liberty to be enjoyed under the gospel.

But not so did prophets and apostles regard the holy law of God. Said David: "I will walk at liberty: for I seek Thy precepts." Psalm 119:45. The apostle James, who wrote after the death of Christ, refers to the Decalogue as "the royal law" and "the perfect law of liberty." James 2:8; 1:25. And the revelator, half a century after the crucifixion, pronounces a blessing upon them "that do His commandments, that they may have right to the tree of life, and may enter in through the gates into the city." Revelation 22:14.

The claim that Christ by His death abolished His Father's law is without foundation. Had it been possible for the law to be changed or set aside, then Christ need not have died to save man from the penalty of sin. The death of Christ, so far from abolishing the law, proves that it is immutable. The Son of God came to "magnify the law, and make it honorable." Isaiah 42:21. He said: "Think not that I am come to destroy the law;" "till heaven and earth pass, one jot or one tittle shall in no wise pass from the law." Matthew 5;17, 18. And concerning Himself He declares: "I delight to do Thy will, O my God: yea, Thy law is within My heart." Psalm 40:8.

The law of God, from its very nature, is unchangeable. It is a revelation of the will and the character of its Author. God is love, and His law is love. Its two great principles are love to God and love to man. "Love is the fulfilling of the law." Romans 13:10. The character of God is righteousness and truth; such is the nature of His law. Says the psalmist: "Thy law is the truth:" "all Thy commandments are righteousness." Psalm 119:142, 172. And the apostle Paul declares: "The law is holy, and the commandment holy, and just, and good." Romans 7:12. Such a law, being an expression of the mind and will of God, must be as enduring as its Author.

It is the work of conversion and sanctification to reconcile men to God by bringing them into accord with the principles of His law. In the beginning, man was created in the image of God. He was in perfect harmony with the nature and the law of God; the principles of righteousness were written upon his heart. But sin alienated him from his Maker. He no longer reflected the divine image. His heart was at war with the principles of God's law. "The carnal mind is enmity against God: for it is not subject to the law of God, neither indeed can be." Romans 8:7. But "God so loved the world, that He gave His only-begotten Son," that man might be reconciled to God. Through the merits of Christ he can be restored to harmony with his Maker. His heart must be renewed by divine grace; he must have a new life from above. This change is the new birth, without which, says Jesus, "he cannot see the kingdom of God."

The first step in reconciliation to God is the conviction of sin. "Sin is the transgression of the law." By the law is the knowledge of sin." 1 John 3:4; Romans 3:20. In order to see his guilt, the sinner must test his character by God's great standard of righteousness. It is a mirror which shows the perfection of a righteous character and enables him to discern the defects in his own.

The law reveals to man his sins, but it provides no remedy. While it promises life to the obedient, it declares that death is the portion of the transgressor. The gospel of Christ alone can free him from the condemnation or the defilement of sin. He must exercise repentance toward God, whose law has been transgressed; and faith in Christ, his atoning sacrifice. Thus he obtains "remission of sins that are past" and becomes a partaker of the divine nature. He is a child of God, having received the spirit of adoption, whereby he cries: "Abba, Father!"

Is he now free to transgress God's law? Says Paul: "Do we then make void the law through faith? God forbid: yea, we establish the law." "How shall we, that are dead to sin, live any longer therein?" And John declares: "This is the love of God, that we keep His commandments: and His commandments are not grievous." Romans 3:31; 6:2; 1 John 5:3. In the new birth the heart is brought into harmony with God, as it is brought into accord with His law. When this mighty change has taken place in the sinner, he has passed from death unto life, from sin unto holiness, from transgression and rebellion to obedience and loyalty. The old life of alienation from God has ended; the new life of reconciliation, of faith and love, has begun. Then "the righteousness of the law" will "be fulfilled in us, who walk not after the flesh, but after the Spirit." Romans 8:4. And the language of the soul will be: "O how love I Thy law! it is my meditation all the day." Psalm 119:97.

"The law of the Lord is perfect, converting the soul." Psalm 19:7. Without the law, men have no just conception of the purity and holiness of God or of their own guilt and uncleanness. They have no true conviction of sin and feel no need of repentance. Not seeing their lost condition as violators of God's law, they do not realize their need of the atoning blood of Christ. The hope of salvation is accepted without a radical change of heart or reformation of life. Thus superficial conversions abound, and multitudes are joined to the church who have never been united to Christ.

Erroneous theories of sanctification, also, springing from neglect or rejection of the divine law, have a prominent place in the religious movements of the day. These theories are both false in doctrine and dangerous in practical results; and the fact that they are so generally finding favor, renders it doubly essential that all have a clear understanding of what the Scriptures teach upon this point.

True sanctification is a Bible doctrine. The apostle Paul, in his letter to the Thessalonian church, declares: "This is the will of God, even your sanctification." And he prays: "The very God of peace sanctify you wholly." 1 Thessalonians 4:3; 5:23. The Bible clearly teaches what sanctification is and how it is to be attained. The Saviour prayed for His disciples: "Sanctify them through Thy truth: Thy word is truth." John 17:17. And Paul teaches that believers are to be "sanctified by the Holy Ghost." Romans 15:16. What is the work of the Holy Spirit? Jesus told His disciples: "When He, the Spirit of truth, is come, He will guide you into all truth." John 16:13. And the psalmist says: "Thy law is the truth." By the word and the Spirit of God are opened to men the great principles of righteousness embodied in His law. And since the law of God is "holy, and just, and good," a transcript of the divine perfection, it follows that a character formed by obedience to that law will be holy. Christ is a perfect example of such a character. He says: "I have kept My Father's commandments." "I do always those things that please Him." John 15:10; 8:29. The followers of Christ are to become like Him—by the grace of God to form characters in harmony with the principles of His holy law. This is Bible sanctification.

This work can be accomplished only through faith in Christ, by the power of the indwelling Spirit of God. Paul admonishes believers: "Work out your own salvation with fear and trembling. For it is God which worketh in you both to will and to do of His good pleasure." Philippians 2:12, 13. The Christian will feel the promptings of sin, but he will maintain a constant warfare against it. Here is where Christ's help is needed. Human weakness becomes united to divine strength, and faith exclaims: "Thanks be to God, which giveth us the victory through our Lord Jesus Christ." 1 Corinthians 15:57.

The Scriptures plainly show that the work of sanctification is progressive. When in conversion the sinner finds peace with God through the blood of the atonement, the Christian life has but just begun. Now he is to "go on unto perfection;" to grow up "unto the measure of the stature of the fullness of Christ." Says the apostle Paul: "This one thing I do, forgetting those things which are behind, and reaching forth unto those things which are before, I press toward the mark for the prize of the high calling of God in Christ Jesus." Philippians 3:13, 14. And Peter sets before us the steps by which Bible sanctification is to be attained: "Giving all diligence, add to your faith virtue; and to virtue knowledge; and to knowledge temperance; and to temperance patience; and to patience godliness; and to godliness brotherly kindness; and to brotherly kindness charity. ... If ye do these things, ye shall never fall." 2 Peter 1:5-10.

Those who experience the sanctification of the Bible will manifest a spirit of humility. Like Moses, they have had a view of the awful majesty of holiness, and they see their own unworthiness in contrast with the purity and exalted perfection of the Infinite One.

The prophet Daniel was an example of true sanctification. His long life was filled up with noble service for his Master. He was a man "greatly beloved" (Daniel 10:11) of Heaven. Yet instead of claiming to be pure and holy, this honored prophet identified himself with the really sinful of Israel as he pleaded before God in behalf of his people: "We do not present our supplications before Thee for our righteousness, but for Thy great mercies." "We have sinned, we have done wickedly." He declares: "I was speaking, and praying, and confessing my sin and the sin of my people." And when at a later time the Son of God appeared, to give him instruction, Daniel says: "My comeliness was turned in me into corruption, and I retained no strength." Daniel 9:18, 15, 20; 10:8.

When Job heard the voice of the Lord out of the whirlwind, he exclaimed: "I abhor myself, and repent in dust and ashes." Job 42:6. It was when Isaiah saw the glory of the Lord, and heard the cherubim crying, "Holy, holy, holy, is the Lord of hosts," that he cried out, "Woe is me! for I am undone." Isaiah 6:3, 5. Paul, after he was caught up into the third heaven and heard things which it was not possible for a man to utter, speaks of himself as "less than the least of all saints." 2 Corinthians 12:2-4, margin; Ephesians 3:8. It was the beloved John, who leaned on Jesus' breast and beheld His glory, that fell as one dead before the feet of the angel. Revelation 1:17.

There can be no self-exaltation, no boastful claim to freedom from sin, on the part of those who walk in the shadow of Calvary's cross. They feel that it was their sin which caused the agony that broke the heart of the Son of God, and this thought will lead them to self-abasement. Those who live nearest to Jesus discern most clearly the frailty and sinfulness of humanity, and their only hope is in the merit of a crucified and risen Saviour.

The sanctification now gaining prominence in the religious world carries with it a spirit of self-exaltation and a disregard for the law of God that mark it as foreign to the religion of the Bible. Its advocates teach that sanctification is an instantaneous work, by which, through faith alone, they attain to perfect holiness. "Only believe," say they, "and the blessing is yours." No further effort on the part of the receiver is supposed to be required. At the same time they deny the authority of the law of God, urging that they are released from obligation to keep the commandments. But is it possible for men to be holy, in accord with the will and character of God, without coming into harmony with the principles which are an expression of His nature and will, and which show what is well pleasing to Him?

The desire for an easy religion that requires no striving, no self-denial, no divorce from the follies of the world, has made the doctrine of faith, and faith only, a popular doctrine; but what saith the word of God? Says the apostle James: "What doth it profit, my brethren, though a man say he hath faith, and have not works? can faith save him? ... Wilt thou know, O vain man, that faith without works is dead? Was not

Abraham our father justified by works, when he had offered Isaac his son upon the altar? Seest thou how faith wrought with his works, and by works was faith made perfect? ... Ye see then how that by works a man is justified, and not by faith only." James 2:14-24.

The testimony of the word of God is against this ensnaring doctrine of faith without works. It is not faith that claims the favor of Heaven without complying with the conditions upon which mercy is to be granted, it is presumption; for genuine faith has its foundation in the promises and provisions of the Scriptures.

Let none deceive themselves with the belief that they can become holy while willfully violating one of God's requirements. The commission of a known sin silences the witnessing voice of the Spirit and separates the soul from God. "Sin is the transgression of the law." And "whosoever sinneth [transgresseth the law] hath not seen Him, neither known Him." 1 John 3:6. Though John in his epistles dwells so fully upon love, yet he does not hesitate to reveal the true character of that class who claim to be sanctified while living in transgression of the law of God. "He that saith, I know Him, and keepeth not His commandments, is a liar, and the truth is not in him. But whoso keepeth His word, in him verily is the love of God perfected." 1 John 2:4, 5. Here is the test of every man's profession. We cannot accord holiness to any man without bringing him to the measurement of God's only standard of holiness in heaven and in earth. If men feel no weight of the moral law, if they belittle and make light of God's precepts, if they break one of the least of these commandments, and teach men so, they shall be of no esteem in the sight of Heaven, and we may know that their claims are without foundation.

And the claim to be without sin is, in itself, evidence that he who makes this claim is far from holy. It is because he has no true conception of the infinite purity and holiness of God or of what they must become who shall be in harmony with His character; because he has no true conception of the purity and exalted loveliness of Jesus, and the malignity and evil of sin, that man can regard himself as holy. The greater the distance between himself and Christ, and the more inadequate his conceptions of the divine character and requirements, the more righteous he appears in his own eyes.

The sanctification set forth in the Scriptures embraces the entire being—spirit, soul, and body. Paul prayed for the Thessalonians that their "whole spirit and soul and body be preserved blameless unto the coming of our Lord Jesus Christ." 1 Thessalonians 5:23. Again he writes to believers: "I beseech you therefore, brethren, by the mercies of God, that ye present your bodies a living sacrifice, holy, acceptable unto God." Romans 12:1. In the time of ancient Israel every offering brought as a sacrifice to God was carefully examined. If any defect was discovered in the animal presented, it was refused; for God had commanded that the offering be "without blemish." So Christians are bidden to present their bodies, "a living sacrifice, holy, acceptable unto God." In order to do this, all their powers must be preserved in the best possible condition. Every practice that weakens physical or mental strength unfits man for the service of his Creator. And will God be pleased with anything less than the best we can offer? Said Christ: "Thou shalt love the Lord thy God with all thy heart." Those who do love God with all the heart will desire to give Him the best service of their life, and they will be constantly seeking to bring every power of their being into harmony with the laws that will promote their ability to do His will. They will not, by the indulgence of appetite or passion, enfeeble or defile the offering which they present to their heavenly Father.

Peter says: "Abstain from fleshly lusts, which war against the soul." 1 Peter 2:11. Every sinful gratification tends to benumb the faculties and deaden the mental and spiritual perceptions, and the word or the Spirit of God can make but a feeble impression upon the heart. Paul writes to the Corinthians: "Let us cleanse ourselves from all filthiness of the flesh and spirit, perfecting holiness in the fear of God." 2 Corinthians 7:1. And with the fruits of the Spirit—"love, joy, peace, long-suffering, gentleness, goodness, faith, meekness"—he classes "temperance." Galatians 5:22, 23.

Notwithstanding these inspired declarations, how many professed Christians are enfeebling their powers in the pursuit of gain or the worship of fashion; how many are debasing their godlike manhood by gluttony, by wine drinking, by forbidden pleasure. And the church, instead of rebuking, too often encourages the evil by appealing to appetite, to desire for gain or love of pleasure, to replenish her treasury, which love for Christ is too feeble to supply. Were Jesus to enter the churches of today and behold the feasting and unholy traffic there conducted in the name of religion, would He not drive out those desecrators, as He banished the money-changers from the temple?

The apostle James declares that the wisdom from above is "first pure." Had he encountered those who take the precious name of Jesus upon lips defiled by tobacco, those whose breath and person are contaminated by its foul odor, and who pollute the air of heaven and force all about them to inhale the poison—had the apostle come in contact with a practice so opposed to the purity of the gospel, would he not have denounced it as "earthly, sensual, devilish"? Slaves of tobacco, claiming the blessing of entire sanctification, talk of their hope of heaven; but God's word plainly declares that "there shall in no wise enter into it anything that defileth." Revelation 21:27.

"Know ye not that your body is the temple of the Holy Ghost which is in you, which ye have of God, and ye are not your own? for ye are bought with a price: therefore glorify God in your body, and in your spirit, which are God's." 1 Corinthians 6:19, 20. He whose body is the temple of the Holy Spirit will not be enslaved by a pernicious habit. His powers belong to Christ, who has bought him with the price of blood. His property is the Lord's. How could he be guiltless in squandering this entrusted capital? Professed Christians yearly expend an immense sum upon useless and pernicious indulgences, while souls are perishing for the word of life. God is robbed in tithes and offerings, while they consume upon the altar of destroying lust more than they give to relieve the poor or for the support of the gospel. If all who profess to be followers of Christ were truly sanctified, their means, instead of being spent for needless and even hurtful indulgences, would be turned into the Lord's treasury, and Christians would set an example of temperance, self-denial, and self-sacrifice. Then they would be the light of the world.

The world is given up to self-indulgence. "The lust of the flesh, and the lust of the eyes, and the pride of life" control the masses of the people. But Christ's followers have a holier calling. "Come out from among them, and be ye separate, saith the Lord, and touch not the unclean." In the light of God's word we are justified in declaring that sanctification cannot be genuine which does not work this utter renunciation of the sinful pursuits and gratifications of the world.

To those who comply with the conditions, "Come out from among them, and be ye separate, … and touch not the unclean," God's promise is, "I will receive you, and will be a Father unto you, and ye shall be My sons and daughters, saith the Lord Almighty." 2 Corinthians 6:17, 18.

It is the privilege and the duty of every Christian to have a rich and abundant experience in the things of God. "I am the light of the world," said Jesus. "He that followeth Me shall not walk in darkness, but shall have the light of life." John 8:12. "The path of the just is as the shining light, that shineth more and more unto the perfect day." Proverbs 4:18. Every step of faith and obedience brings the soul into closer connection with the Light of the world, in whom there "is no darkness at all." The bright beams of the Sun of Righteousness shine upon the servants of God, and they are to reflect His rays. As the stars tell us that there is a great light in heaven with whose glory they are made bright, so Christians are to make it manifest that there is a God on the throne of the universe whose character is worthy of praise and imitation. The graces of His Spirit, the purity and holiness of His character, will be manifest in His witnesses.

Paul in his letter to the Colossians sets forth the rich blessings granted to the children of God. He says: We "do not cease to pray for you, and to desire that ye might be filled with the knowledge of His will in all wisdom and spiritual understanding; that ye might walk worthy of the Lord unto all pleasing, being fruitful in every good work, and increasing in the knowledge of God; strengthened with all might, according to His glorious power, unto all patience and long-suffering with joyfulness." Colossians 1:9-11.

Again he writes of his desire that the brethren at Ephesus might come to understand the height of the Christian's privilege. He opens before them, in the most comprehensive language, the marvelous power and knowledge that they might possess as sons and daughters of the Most High. It was theirs "to be strengthened with might by His Spirit in the inner man," to be "rooted and grounded in love," to comprehend with all saints what is the breadth, and length, and depth, and height; and to know the love of Christ, which passeth knowledge." But the prayer of the apostle reaches the climax of privilege when he prays that "ye might be filled with all the fullness of God." Ephesians 3:16-19.

Here are revealed the heights of attainment that we may reach through faith in the promises of our heavenly Father, when we fulfill His requirements. Through the merits of Christ we have access to the throne of Infinite Power. "He that spared not His own Son, but delivered Him up for us all, how shall He not with Him also freely give us all things?" Romans 8:32. The Father gave His Spirit without measure to His Son, and we also may partake of its fullness. Jesus says, "If ye then, being evil, know how to give good gifts unto your children: how much more shall your heavenly Father give the Holy Spirit to them that ask Him?" Luke 11:13. "If ye shall ask anything in My name, I will do it." "Ask, and ye shall receive, that your joy may be full." John 14:14, 16:24.

While the Christian's life will be characterized by humility, it should not be marked with sadness and self-depreciation. It is the privilege of everyone so to live that God will approve and bless him. It is not the will of our heavenly Father that we should be ever under condemnation and darkness. There is no evidence of true humility in going with the head bowed down and the heart filled with thoughts of self. We may go to Jesus and be cleansed, and stand before the law without shame and remorse. "There is therefore now no condemnation to them which are in Christ Jesus, who walk not after the flesh, but after the Spirit." Romans 8:1.

Through Jesus the fallen sons of Adam become "sons of God." "Both He that sanctifieth and they who are sanctified are all of one: for which cause He is not ashamed to call them brethren." Hebrews 2:11. The Christian's life should be one of faith, of victory, and joy in God. "Whatsoever is born of God overcometh the world: and this is the victory that overcometh the world, even our faith." I John 5:4. Truly spoke God's servant Nehemiah: "The *joy* of the Lord is your strength." Nehemiah 8:10. And Paul says: "Rejoice in the Lord alway: and again I say, Rejoice." "Rejoice evermore. Pray without ceasing. In everything give thanks: for this is the will of God in Christ Jesus concerning you." Philippians 4:4; 1 Thessalonians 5:16-18.

Such are the fruits of Bible conversion and sanctification; and it is because the great principles of righteousness set forth in the law of God are so indifferently regarded by the Christian world that these fruits are so rarely witnessed. This is why there is manifest so little of that deep, abiding work of the Spirit of God which marked revivals in former years.

It is by beholding that we become changed. And as those sacred precepts in which God has opened to men the perfection and holiness of His character are neglected, and the minds of the people are attracted to human teachings and theories, what marvel that there has followed a decline of living piety in the church. Saith the Lord: "They have forsaken Me the fountain of living waters, and hewed them out cisterns, broken cisterns, that can hold no water." Jeremiah 2:13.

"Blessed is the man that walketh not in the counsel of the ungodly. … But his delight is in the law of the Lord; and in His law doth he meditate day and night. And he shall be like a tree planted by the rivers of water, that bringeth forth his fruit in his season; his leaf also shall not wither; and whatsoever he doeth shall prosper." Psalm 1:1-3. It is only as the law of God is restored to its rightful position that there can be a revival of primitive faith and godliness among His professed people. "Thus saith the Lord, Stand ye in the ways, and see, and ask for the old paths, where is the good way, and walk therein, and ye shall find rest for your souls." Jeremiah 6:16.

Complete Your Set!

Book One	Book Two	Book Three	Book Four

| God's Holy Word | America in Prophecy | Cracking the Code | The World Out of Control |

As the world buckles under the weight of catastrophe—9/11, the great tsunami, earthquakes, forest fires, and wave after wave of hurricanes—this book reveals that these are but a fraction of the destructive forces that are yet to come. With so many crises—the ongoing war on terror; an increase in brutal crimes, especially against children; economic and political instability; lawlessness and confusion; and the proliferation and acceptance of immorality—mainstream, secular media outlets are asking, "Is this the end of the world?"

The key to answering this question is looking into a long-forgotten past. In this classic masterpiece by one of the world's most influential writers, you'll begin to understand the cataclysmic events battering our world in a new light. You'll see how and why history repeats itself, yet more dangerously than in previous times.

So different than anything you've ever read, but authenticated by hundreds of Bible verses and keen insight, This set is an eye-opening journey through human history and beyond that plunges you headfirst into the ultimate battle between good and evil.

Special Edition Complete Series

This special edition book contains all four books of the series under one cover. This must-read masterpiece has given knowledge and assurance to millions. Now it's your turn to have the answers you need to face the future.